Henry Schwing

The Woman's Hymnal

A Collection of Sacred Lyrics Set to Music and Arranged as Duets...

Henry Schwing

The Woman's Hymnal
A Collection of Sacred Lyrics Set to Music and Arranged as Duets...

ISBN/EAN: 9783744783712

Printed in Europe, USA, Canada, Australia, Japan

Cover: Foto ©Thomas Meinert / pixelio.de

More available books at **www.hansebooks.com**

THE WOMAN'S HYMNAL.

A

COLLECTION OF SACRED LYRICS SET TO MUSIC

AND

ARRANGED AS DUETS FOR SOPRANO AND ALTO, (TENOR AND BASS AD LIBITUM.)

FOR THE USE OF

THE WOMAN'S COLLEGE OF BALTIMORE.

BY

HENRY SCHWING,

INSTRUCTOR IN THEORY OF MUSIC.

PUBLISHED BY THE COLLEGE.
1892.

Copyright, 1892, by

THE WOMAN'S COLLEGE OF BALTIMORE, MD.

NOTICE. — All the music in this collection, having been specially arranged by the Editor in the form described on the title page and in the preface, is strictly copyright and cannot be used without permission.

MANUFACTURED BY F. H. GILSON COMPANY, BOSTON.

PREFACE.

The daily exercises of the Women's College of Baltimore are preceded by a brief chapel-service. In order to add effectiveness to the singing it was deemed suitable that the music used should be arranged especially for female voices. In this book standard tunes are written as duets for soprano and alto as complete as is possible in two-part composition. At the same time, in order to widen the sphere of its usefulness, tenor and bass have been added. The music as it stands may be sung in the following four ways,—

1. Duets for soprano and alto.

2. Trios for soprano and two altos the second alto singing the bass part, which of course, sounds one octave higher.

3. Trios for soprano, alto and bass.

4. Quartets for soprano, alto, tenor and bass.

It will be noticed that in a few instances the second alto will sing higher than the soprano; this will not occasion discord.

This collection may be used in Sunday schools, the girls singing the soprano, the boys the alto and the male teachers the tenor and bass.

Accompanists will sometimes be compelled to omit the tenor, which is occasionally beyond the reach of either hand.

It may be added that in addition to old favorites this book contains many gems from the great masters arranged especially for this work.

SEPTEMBER, 1891.   H. S.

THE WOMAN'S HYMNAL.

No. 1.   ST. AGNES. C. M.

Rev. J. B. Dykes (1823—1876).

1 Workman of God! O lose not heart,
   But learn what God is like;
   And in the darkest battle-field
   Thou shalt know where to strike.

2 Thrice blest is he to whom is given
   The instinct that can tell
   That God is on the field, when He
   Is most invisible.

3 Blest too is he who can divine
   Where real right doth lie,
   And dares to take the side that seems
   Wrong to man's blindfold eye.

4 Then learn to scorn the praise of men,
   And learn to lose with God;
   For Jesus won the world through shame,
   And beckons thee His road.

Rev. Frederick W. Faber (1815—1863).

No. 2. ANTIOCH. C. M.

G. F. Handel (1685—1759).

1 Joy to the world! the Lord is come;
  Let earth receive her King;
  Let every heart prepare Him room,
  ‖: And heaven and nature sing.:‖

2 Joy to the world! the Saviour reigns;
  Let men their songs employ;
  While fields and floods, rocks, hills and
  ‖: Repeat the sounding joy.:‖ [plains

3 No more let sin and sorrow grow,
  Nor thorns infest the ground;
  He comes to make His blessings flow
  ‖: Far as the curse is found.:‖

4 He rules the world with truth and grace,
  And makes the nations prove
  The glories of His righteousness,
  ‖: And wonders of His love.:‖

Rev. Isaac Watts, D. D. (1674—1748).

No. 3. ARLINGTON. C. M.

TH. A. ARNE (1710—1778).

1 There is an eye that never sleeps
    Beneath the wing of night;
  There is an ear that never shuts,
    When sink the beams of light.

2 There is an arm that never tires,
    When human strength gives way;
  There is a love that never fails,
    When earthly loves decay.

3 That eye is fixed on seraph throngs;
    That arm upholds the sky;
  That ear is filled with angel songs;
    That love is throned on high.

4 But there's a power which man can wield,
    When mortal aid is vain,
  That eye, that arm, that love to reach,
    That listening ear to gain.

5 That power is prayer, which soars on high,
    Through Jesus, to the throne,
  And moves the hand which moves the world,
    To bring salvation down.

JOHN A. WALLACE (1802—1870).

No. 4. AZMON. C. M.

C. G. Glaser (1784 — 1829).

1 O for a heart to praise my God,
   A heart from sin set free!
  A heart that always feels thy blood,
   So freely spilt for me.

2 A heart resigned, submissive, meek,
   My great Redeemer's throne;
  Where only Christ is heard to speak,
   Where Jesus reigns alone.

3 O for a lowly, contrite heart,
   Believing, true and clean,
  Which neither life, nor death can part
   From him that dwells within!

4 A heart in every thought renewed,
   And full of love divine;
  Perfect, and right, and pure, and good,
   A copy, Lord, of thine.

5 Thy nature, gracious Lord, impart;
   Come quickly from above:
  Write thy new name upon my heart,
   Thy new, best name of love.

Charles Wesley (1708 — 1788).

(8)

No. 5   BALERMA. C. M.

Scotch Air.

1 O Sun of righteousness, arise
   With healing in thy wing!
   To my diseased, my fainting soul,
   Life and salvation bring.

2 These clouds of pride and sin dispel,
   By thy all-piercing beam;
   Lighten mine eyes with faith; my heart
   With holy hope inflame;

3 My mind, by thy all-quickening power,
   From low desires set free;
   Unite my scattered thoughts, and fix
   My love entire on Thee.

4 Nothing I ask or want beside,
   Of all in earth or heaven,
   But let me feel thy blood applied,
   And live and die forgiven.

CHARLES WESLEY (1708—1788).

No. 6.   BARBY. C. M.

W. Tansur (1700—1783).

1 There is a safe and secret place
   Beneath the wings divine,
   Reserved for all the heirs of grace;
   O be that refuge mine!

2 The least and feeblest there may bide,
   Uninjured and unawed;
   While thousands fall on every side,
   He rests secure in God.

3 He feeds in pastures large and fair
   Of love and truth divine;
   O child of God, O glory's heir,
   How rich a lot is thine!

4 A hand almighty to defend,
   An ear for every call,
   An honored life, a peaceful end,
   And heaven to crown it all!

Rev. Henry F. Lyte (1793—1847).

No. 7.   CORONATION. C. M.

O. HOLDEN (1765—1844).

1 All hail the power of Jesus' name!
   Let angels prostrate fall;
   Bring forth the royal diadem,
   And crown him Lord of all.

2 Sinners, whose love can ne'er forget
   The wormwood and the gall;
   Go, spread your trophies at his feet,
   And crown him Lord of all.

3 Let every kindred, every tribe,
   On this terrestrial ball,
   To him all majesty ascribe,
   And crown him Lord of all.

4 Oh, that with yonder sacred throng
   We at his feet may fall!
   We'll join the everlasting song,
   And crown him Lord of all.

Rev. EDWARD PERRONET (—1792).

No. 8. COVENTRY. C. M.

1 The glorious universe around,
   The heavens with all their train,
  Sun, moon, and stars, are firmly bound
   In one mysterious chain.

2 In one fraternal bond of love,
   One fellowship of mind,
  The saints below and saints above
   Their bliss and glory find.

3 Here, in their house of pilgrimage,
   Thy statutes are their song;
  There, through one bright, eternal age,
   Thy praises they prolong.

4 Lord, may our union form a part
   Of that thrice happy whole;
  Derive its pulse from thee, the heart,
   Its life, from thee, the soul.

(12)   JAMES MONTGOMERY (1771 — 1854).

No. 9. DUNDEE. C. M.

G. Franc (1520 — 1570).

1 God moves in a mysterious way
    His wonders to perform;
  He plants his footsteps in the sea,
    And rides upon the storm.

2 Deep in unfathomable mines
    Of never-failing skill,
  He treasures up his bright designs,
    And works his sovereign will.

3 His purposes will ripen fast,
    Unfolding every hour;
  The bud may have a bitter taste,
    But sweet will be the flower.

4 Blind unbelief is sure to err,
    And scan his work in vain;
  God is his own interpreter,
    And he will make it plain.

William Cowper (1731 — 1800).

No. 10.   HEIDELBERG. C. M.

1 Walk in the light! so shalt thou know
   That fellowship of love,
   His Spirit only can bestow
   Who reigns in light above.

2 Walk in the light! and thou shalt find
   Thy heart made truly his,
   Who dwells in cloudless light enshrined,
   In whom no darkness is.

3 Walk in the light! and thou shalt own
   Thy darkness passed away,
   Because that light hath on thee shone
   In which is perfect day.

4 Walk in the light! thy path shall be
   Peaceful, serene, and bright;
   For God, by grace, shall dwell in thee,
   And God himself is light.
                        BERNARD BARTON (1784—1849).

No. 11.   HOLY CROSS. C. M.

UNKNOWN.

1 O Jesus, King most wonderful,
    Thou Conqueror renowned,
  Thou sweetness most ineffable,
    In whom all joys are found!

2 When once thou visitest the heart,
    Then truth begins to shine,
  Then earthly vanities depart,
    Then kindles love divine.

3 Jesus, may all confess thy name,
    Thy wondrous love adore,
  And, seeking thee, themselves inflame
    To seek thee more and more.

4 Thee, Jesus, may our voices bless;
    Thee may we love alone;
  And ever in our lives express,
    The image of thine own.

BERNARD of CLAIRVAUX (1091—1153), tr. by E. CASWALL.

No. 12.   LANESBORO.   C. M.

ENGLISH TUNE.

1 Jesus, the very thought of thee
   With sweetness fills the breast;
   : But sweeter far thy face to see,:
   And in thy presence rest.

2 O Hope of every contrite heart,
   O Joy of all the meek,
   : To those who ask, how kind thou art!:
   How good to those who seek!

3 But what to those who find? Ah, this
   Nor tongue nor pen can show;
   : The love of Jesus, what it is,:
   None but his loved ones know.

4 Jesus, our only joy be thou,
   As thou our prize wilt be;
   : In thee be all our glory now,:
   And through eternity.

BERNARD of CLAIRVAUX (1091—1153), tr. by E. CASWALL.

No. 13.   MANOAH.   C. M.

1 We may not climb the heavenly steeps
    To bring the Lord Christ down;
  In vain we search the lowest deeps,
    For him no depths can drown.

2 But warm, sweet, tender, even yet
    A present help is he;
  And faith has yet its Olivet,
    And love its Galilee.

3 The healing of the seamless dress
    Is by our beds of pain;
  We touch him in life's throng and press,
    And we are whole again.

4 Through him the first fond prayers are said
    Our lips of childhood frame;
  The last low whispers of our dead
    Are burdened with his name.

5 O Lord and Master of us all,
    Whate'er our name or sign,
  We own thy sway, we hear thy call,
    We test our lives by thine!

            JOHN G. WHITTIER, 1868.

(17)

No. 14. ST. MARTIN'S. C. M.

WILLIAM TANSUR (1700—1783).

1 As shadows, cast by cloud and sun,
   Flit o'er the summer grass,
   So, in thy sight, Almighty One,
   Earth's generations pass.

2 And as the years, an endless host,
   Come swiftly pressing on,
   The brightest names that earth can boast
   Just glisten and are gone.

3 Yet doth the star of Bethlehem shed
   A lustre pure and sweet;
   And still it leads, as once it led,
   To the Messiah's feet.

4 O Father, may that holy star
   Grow every year more bright,
   And send its glorious beams afar
   To fill the world with light.

WILLIAM C. BRYANT (1794—1878).

No. 15. MEAR. C. M.
WELSH AIR.

1 Oh, it is hard to work for God,
 To rise and take his part
Upon this battle-field of earth,
 And not sometimes lose heart!

2 He hides himself so wondrously,
 As though there were no God;
He is least seen when all the powers
 Of ill are most abroad;

3 Or he deserts us in the hour
 The fight is all but lost;
And seems to leave us to ourselves
 Just when we need him most.

4 It is not so, but so it looks;
 And we lose courage then;
And doubts will come if God hath kept
 His promises to men.

5 But right is right, since God is God;
 And right the day must win;
To doubt would be disloyalty,
 To falter would be sin!

Rev. FREDERICK W. FABER, D. D. (1815 – 1863).

No. 16.   MOZART. C. M.

W. A. Mozart (1756—1791).

1 The counsels of redeeming grace
  The sacred leaves unfold;
  And here the Saviour's lovely face
  Our raptured eyes behold.

2 Here light descending from above
  Directs our doubtful feet;
  Here promises of heavenly love
  Our ardent wishes meet.

3 Our numerous griefs are here redressed,
  And all our wants supplied;
  Naught we can ask to make us blest
  Is in this book denied.

4 For these inestimable gains,
  That so enrich the mind,
  O, may we search with eager pains,
  Assured that we shall find.

Rev. Samuel Stennett, D. D. (1727—1795).

No. 17.   SHONTZ. C. M.
UNKNOWN.

1 Prayer is the breath of God in man,
    Returning whence it came;
  Love is the sacred fire within,
    And prayer the rising flame.

2 It gives the burdened spirit ease,
    And soothes the troubled breast;
  Yields comfort to the mourners here,
    And to the weary rest.

3 When God inclines the heart to pray,
    He hath an ear to hear;
  To him there's music in a groan,
    And beauty in a tear.

4 The humble suppliant cannot fail
    To have his wants supplied,
  Since He for sinners intercedes,
    Who once for sinners died.

BENJAMIN BEDDOME.

No. 18.   NAOMI. C. M.
H. G. NÄGELI (1768—1836).

1 Lord, as to thy dear cross we flee,
   And pray to be forgiven,
  So let thy life our pattern be,
   And form our souls for heaven.

2 Help us, through good report and ill,
   Our daily cross to bear,
  Like thee, to do our Father's will,
   Our brother's griefs to share.

3 Let grace our selfishness expel,
   Our earthliness refine;

And kindness in our bosoms dwell,
 As free and true as thine.

4 If joy shall at thy bidding fly,
   And grief's dark day come on,
  We, in our turn, would meekly cry,
   "Father, thy will be done."

5 Kept peaceful in the midst of strife,
   Forgiving and forgiven,
  O may we lead the pilgrim's life,
   And follow thee to heaven!

Rev. JOHN H. GURNEY (1802—1862).

No. 19.   SALVATION. C. M. Double.
J. N. HUMMEL (1778—1837).

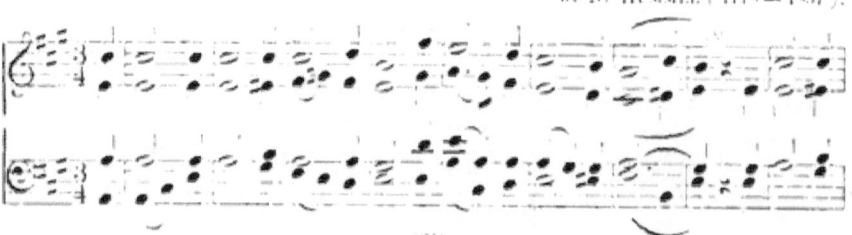

1 My Saviour, on the word of truth
   In earnest hope I live;
I ask for all the precious things,
   Thy boundless love can give.
I look for many a lesser light
   About my path to shine;
But chiefly long to walk with thee,
   And only trust in thine.

2 Thou knowest that I am not blest
   As thou wouldst have me be,
Till all the peace and joy of faith
   Possess my soul in thee;
And still I seek, 'mid many fears,
   With yearnings unexpressed,
The comfort of thy strengthening love,
   Thy soothing, settling rest.

3 It is not as thou wilt with me,
   Till, humbled in the dust,
I know no place in all my heart
   Wherein to put my trust:
Until I find, O Lord, in thee,
   The Lowly and the Meek,
The fullness which thy own redeemed
   Go nowhere else to seek.

                  ANNA L. WARING, 1850.

No. 20.   SIMPSON.   C. M.

L. Spohr (1784—1859).

1 Thou art the Way: — to thee alone
  From sin and death we flee;
  And he who would the Father seek,
  Must seek Him, Lord, by thee.

2 Thou art the Truth: — thy word alone
  True wisdom can impart;
  Thou only canst inform the mind,
  And purify the heart.

3 Thou art the Life: the rending tomb
  Proclaims thy conquering arm;
  And those who put their trust in thee,
  Nor death nor hell shall harm.

4 Thou art the Way, the Truth, the Life;
  Grant us that Way to know,
  That Truth to keep, that Life to win,
  Whose joys eternal flow.

Bishop GEORGE W. DOANE, D. D. (1799—1859).

No. 21.   SPOHR. C. M. Double.
                                         L. Spohr (1784—1859).

) I heard the voice of Jesus say,
   "Come unto me and rest;
Lay down, thou weary one, lay down
   Thy head upon my breast!"
I came to Jesus as I was,
   Weary, and worn, and sad;
I found in him a resting-place,
   And he hath made me glad.

2 I heard the voice of Jesus say
   "Behold, I freely give
The living water; thirsty one,
   Stoop down, and drink, and live!"

I came to Jesus, and I drank
   Of that life-giving stream;
My thirst was quenched, my soul revived,
   And now I live in him.

3 I heard the voice of Jesus say,
   "I am this dark world's Light;
Look unto me, thy morn shall rise
   And all thy day be bright!"
I looked to Jesus, and I found
   In him, my Star, my Sun;
And in that light of life I'll walk,
   Till all my journey's done.
      Rev. HORATIUS BONAR D. D. (1808—).

No. 22.   WARWICK. C. M.

G. Stanley (1767—1822).

1 Lord, in the morning thou shalt hear
    My voice ascending high;
  To thee will I direct my prayer,
    To thee lift up mine eye;

2 Up to the hills where Christ is gone,
    To plead for all his saints,
  Presenting, at the Father's throne,
    Our songs and our complaints.

3 Thou art a God before whose sight
    The wicked shall not stand;
  Sinners shall ne'er be thy delight,
    Nor dwell at thy right hand.

4 O may thy Spirit guide my feet
    In ways of righteousness;
  Make every path of duty straight,
    And plain before my face.

Rev. Isaac Watts, D. D. (1674—1748).

No. 23. ZERAH. C. M.

1 Let every tongue thy goodness speak,
   Thou sovereign Lord of all;
   |: Thy strengthening hands uphold the weak,
   And raise the poor that fall. :||

2 When sorrows bow the spirit down,
   When virtue lies distressed.
   |: Beneath the proud oppressor's frown,
   Thou giv'st the mourner rest. :||

3 Thou know'st the pains thy servants feel,
   Thou hear'st thy children's cry;
   |: And their best wishes to fulfill,
   Thy grace is ever nigh. :||

4 Thy mercy never shall remove
   From men of heart sincere;
   |: Thou sav'st the souls whose humble love
   Is joined with holy fear. :||

Rev. Isaac Watts, D. D. (1674—1748).

No. 24. DUKE STREET. L. M.

J. HATTON (—1793).

1 It may not be our lot to wield
  The sickle in the ripened field;
  Nor ours to hear, on summer eves,
  The reaper's song among the sheaves.

2 Yet where our duty's task is wrought
  In unison with God's great thought,
  The near and future blend in one,
  And whatsoe'er is willed, is done.

3 And ours the grateful service whence
  Comes, day by day, the recompense;
  The hope, the trust, the purpose stayed,
  The fountain, and the noonday shade.

4 And were this life the utmost span,
  The only end and aim of man,
  Better the toil of fields like these
  Than waking dream and slothful ease.

5 But life, though failing like our grain,
  Like that revives and springs again;
  And, early called, how blest are they
  Who wait in heaven, their harvest day!

JOHN G. WHITTIER 1808—).

No. 25.   GERMANY. L. M.

L. v. BEETHOVEN (1770—1827).

1 Jesus, my Advocate above,
   My Friend before the throne of love,
   If now for me prevails thy prayer,
   If now I find thee pleading there,—

2 If thou the secret wish convey,
   And sweetly prompt my heart to pray,—
   Hear, and my weak petitions join,
   Almighty Advocate, to thine.

3 Jesus, my heart's desire obtain;
   My earnest suit present and gain:
   My fullness of corruption show;
   The knowledge of myself bestow.

4 O sovereign Love, to thee I cry,
   Give me thyself, or else I die!
   Save me from death, from hell set free;
   Death, hell, are but the want of thee.

              Rev. CHARLES WESLEY (1708—1788).

No. 26. HAMBURG. L. M.

From a Gregorian Chant.

1 Holy as thou, O Lord, is none;
  Thy holiness is all thine own;
  A drop of that unbounded sea
  Is ours, — a drop derived from thee.

2 And when thy purity we share,
  Thine only glory we declare;
  And, humbled into nothing, own,
  Holy and pure is God alone.

3 Sole, self-existing God and Lord,
  By all thy heavenly hosts adored,
  Let all on earth bow down to thee,
  And own thy peerless majesty.

4 Thy power unparalleled confess,
  Established on the rock of peace;
  The rock that never shall remove,
  The rock of pure almighty love.

Rev. CHARLES WESLEY (1708 — 1788).

No. 27.   ST. HELEN. L. M.

L. v. Beethoven (1770 – 1827).

1 New every morning is the love
   Our wakening and uprising prove;
   Through sleep and darkness safely brought,
   Restored to life, and power, and thought.

2 New mercies, each returning day,
   Hover around us while we pray:
   New perils past, new sins forgiven,
   New thoughts of God, new hopes of heaven.

3 If on our daily course our mind
   Be set to hallow all we find,
   New treasures still of countless price
   God will provide for sacrifice.

4 The trivial round, the common task,
   Will furnish all we ought to ask,—
   Room to deny ourselves, a road
   To bring us daily nearer God.

5 Only, O Lord, in thy dear love
   Fit us for perfect rest above;
   And help us this, and every day,
   To live more nearly as we pray.

Rev. John Keble (1792 – 1866).

(31)

No. 28.   HOPE. L. M.

FELIX MENDELSSOHN (1809—1847).

1 Jesus, the sinner's Friend, to thee,
  Lost and undone, for aid I flee,
  Weary of earth, myself and sin;
  Open thine arms, and take me in.

2 Pity and heal my sin-sick soul;
  'Tis thou alone canst make me whole;
  Dark, till in me thine image shine,
  And lost, I am, till thou art mine.

3 At last I own it cannot be
  That I should fit myself for thee;
  Here, then, to thee I all resign;
  Thine is the work, and only thine.

4 What shall I say thy grace to move?
  Lord, I am sin — but thou art love:
  I give up every plea beside —
  Lord, I am lost — but thou hast died.

Rev. CHARLES WESLEY (1708—1788).

(32)

No. 29.   HURSLEY. L. M.
MEL. P. RITTER (1760—1846).

1 Lord of all being! throned afar,
  Thy glory flames from sun and star;
  Center and soul of every sphere,
  Yet to each loving heart how near!

2 Sun of our life, thy quickening ray
  Sheds on our path the glow of day;
  Star of our hope, thy softened light
  Cheers the long watches of the night.

3 Our midnight is thy smile withdrawn;
  Our noon-tide is thy gracious dawn;
  Our rainbow arch thy mercy's sign;
  All, save the clouds of sin are thine!

4 Lord of all life, below, above,
  Whose light is truth, whose warmth is love,
  Before thy ever-blazing throne
  We ask no luster of our own.

5 Grant us thy truth to make us free,
  And kindling hearts that burn for thee,
  Till all thy living altars claim
  One holy light, one heavenly flame.

OLIVER W. HOLMES (1809—).

No. 30. LOUVAN. L. M.

V. C. Taylor (1847—).

1 Lift up your heads, ye mighty gates!
Behold, the King of glory waits;
The King of kings is drawing near,
The Saviour of the world is here.

2 Fling wide the portals of your heart;
Make it a temple, set apart
From earthly use for heaven's employ,
Adorned with prayer, and love, and joy.

3 Redeemer, come! I open wide
My heart to thee: here, Lord, abide!
Let me thy inner presence feel,
Thy grace and love in me reveal!

4 So come, my Sovereign! enter in,
Let new and nobler life begin;
Thy Holy Spirit guide us on,
Until the glorious crown be won!

Rev. Georg Weissel (1590—1635), tr. by Miss C. Winkworth.

No. 31.   MENDON. L. M.
                                              German.

1 Happy the man who finds the grace,
  The blessing of God's chosen race,
  The wisdom coming from above,
  The faith that sweetly works by love.

2 Wisdom divine! who tells the price
  Of wisdom's costly merchandise?
  Wisdom to silver we prefer,
  And gold is dross compared to her.

3 Her hands are filled with length of days,
  True riches, and immortal praise;
  Her ways are ways of pleasantness,
  And all her flowery paths are peace.

4 Happy the man who wisdom gains;
  Thrice happy, who his guest retains:
  He owns, and shall forever own,
  Wisdom, and Christ, and heaven, are one.

                    Rev. CHARLES WESLEY (1708–1788).

No. 32.   MERCY-SEAT. L. M.
German.

1 From every stormy wind that blows,
  From every swelling tide of woes,
  There is a calm, a sure retreat:
  ‖: 'Tis found beneath the mercy-seat.:‖

2 There is a place where Jesus sheds
  The oil of gladness on our heads;
  A place than all besides more sweet;
  ‖: It is the blood-bought mercy-seat :‖

3 There is a scene where spirits blend,
  Where friend holds fellowship with friend;
  Though sundered far, by faith they meet
  ‖: Around one common mercy-seat :‖

4 Ah! whither could we flee for aid,
  When tempted, desolate, dismayed;
  Or how the hosts of hell defeat,
  ‖: Had suffering saints no mercy-seat ?:‖

5 There, there on eagle wings we soar,
  And sin and sense molest no more;
  And heaven comes down our souls to greet,
  ‖: While glory crowns the mercy-seat.:‖

Rev. HUGH STOWELL (1799 – 1865).

No. 33. WILMAN. L. M.

Arr. from BEETHOVEN (1770—1827).

1 Blest hour, when mortal man retires
  To hold communion with his God;
  To send to Heaven his warm desires,
  ‖:And listen to the sacred word.:‖

2 Blest hour, when God himself draws nigh,
  Well pleased his people's voice to hear;
  To hush the penitential sigh,
  ‖:And wipe away the mourner's tear.:‖

3 Blest hour, for, where the Lord resorts,
  Foretastes of future bliss are given;
  And mortals find his earthly courts
  ‖:The house of God, the gate of heaven.:‖

4 Hail, peaceful hour! supremely blest
  Amid the hours of worldly care;
  The hour that yields the spirit rest,
  ‖:That sacred hour, the hour of prayer.:‖

5 And when my hours of prayer are past,
  And this frail tenement decays,
  Then may I spend in heaven at last
  ‖:A never-ending hour of praise.:‖

Rev. THOMAS RAFFLES, D. D. (1788—1863).

No. 34. OLD HUNDRED.

G. Franc (1520—1570).

1 Before Jehovah's awful throne,
  Ye nations bow with sacred joy;
  Know that the Lord is God alone,
  He can create, and he destroy.

2 His sovereign power, without our aid,
  Made us of clay, and formed us men;
  And when like wandering sheep we strayed,
  He brought us to his fold again.

3 We'll crowd thy gates with thankful songs,
  High as the heavens our voices raise;
  And earth, with her ten thousand tongues,
  Shall fill thy courts with sounding praise.

4 Wide as the world is thy command;
  Vast as eternity thy love;
  Firm as a rock thy truth shall stand,
  When rolling years shall cease to move.

Rev. Isaac Watts (1797—1876), alt. by J. Wesley.

No. 35.   PARK STREET. L. M.

F. M. A. VENNA (1788—).

1 Jesus, thou joy of loving hearts!
  Thou Fount of life! thou Light of men!
  From the best bliss that earth imparts,
  ‖: We turn unfilled to thee again.:‖

2 Thy truth unchanged hath ever stood;
  Thou savest those that on thee call;
  To them that seek thee, thou art good,
  ‖: To them that find thee, all in all.:‖

3 We taste thee, O thou Living Bread,
  And long to feast upon thee still;

  We drink of thee, the Fountain Head,
  ‖: And thirst our souls from thee to fill!:‖

4 Our restless spirits yearn for thee,
  Where'er our changeful lot is cast;
  Glad, when thy gracious smile we see,
  ‖: Blest, when our faith can hold thee fast.:‖

5 O Jesus, ever with us stay;
  Make all our moments calm and bright;
  Chase the dark night of sin away,
  ‖: Shed o'er the world thy holy light.:‖

BERNARD OF CLAIRVAUX (1091 – 1153), tr. by R. PALMER.

No. 36.   PRAISE. L. M.

K. KREUZER (1782—).

1 Thou Lamb of God, thou Prince of Peace,
   For thee my thirsty soul doth pine;
   My longing heart implores thy grace;
   O make me in thy likeness shine.

2 When pain o'er my weak flesh prevails,
   With lamb-like patience arm my breast;
   When grief my wounded soul assails,
   In lowly meekness may I rest.

3 Close by thy side still may I keep,
   Howe'er life's various currents flow;
   With steadfast eye mark every step,
   And follow thee where'er thou go.

4 Thou, Lord, the dreadful fight hast won;
   Alone thou hast the wine-press trod;
   In me thy strengthening grace be shown;
   O may I conquer through thy blood.

5 So, when on Zion thou shalt stand,
   And all heaven's host adore their King,
   Shall I be found at thy right hand,
   And, free from pain, thy glories sing.

Rev. C. F. RICHTER. D. D. (1676—1711), tr. by J. WESLEY.

No. 37.   PROMISE. L. M.

F. H. Barthelemon (1741—1808).

1 O God, to thee we raise our eyes;
  Calm resignation we implore;
  O let no murmuring thought arise,
  But humbly let us still adore.

2 With meek submission may we bear
  Each needful cross thou shalt ordain;
  Nor think our trials too severe,
  Nor dare thy justice to arraign.

3 For though mysterious now thy ways
  To erring mortals may appear,
  Hereafter we thy name shall praise,
  For all our keenest sufferings here.

4 Thy needful help, O God, afford,
  Nor let us sink in deep despair;
  Aid us to trust thy sacred word,
  And find our sweetest comfort there.

Charlotte Richardson (1806—).

No. 38.   REMINISCENCE. L. M.

H. SANDERS.

1 O Christ, who hast prepared a place
  For us around thy throne of grace,
  We pray thee, lift our hearts above,
  And draw them with the cords of love.

2 Source of all good, thou, gracious Lord,
  Art our exceeding great reward;
  How transient is our present pain,
  How boundless our eternal gain!

3 With open face and joyful heart,
  We then shall see thee as thou art:
  Our love shall never cease to glow,
  Our praise shall never cease to flow.

4 Thy never-failing grace to prove,
  A surety of thine endless love,
  Send down thy Holy Ghost, to be
  The raiser of our souls to thee.

SANTOLIUS VICTORINUS (1630—1697), tr. by J. CHANDLER.

No. 39.   SHEFLOE. L. M. 6 lines.

F. Mendelssohn (1809 — 1847).

1. My hope is built on nothing less
   Than Jesus' blood and righteousness;
   I dare not trust the sweetest frame,
   But wholly lean on Jesus' name:
   On Christ, the solid rock, I stand;
   All other ground is sinking sand.

2. When darkness seems to veil his face,
   I rest on his unchanging grace;
   In every high and stormy gale,
   My anchor holds within the veil:
   On Christ, the solid rock, I stand;
   All other ground is sinking sand.

3. His oath, his covenant, and blood,
   Support me in the whelming flood:
   When all around my soul gives way,
   He then is all my hope and stay:
   On Christ, the solid rock I stand;
   All other ground is sinking sand.

Rev. Edward Mote (1797 —).

No. 40.   SPENCER. L. M.

Arr. from F. Mendelssohn (1809—1847).

1 O come, Creator Spirit blest!
  Within these souls of thine to rest;
  Come, with thy grace and heavenly aid,
  To fill the hearts which thou hast made.

2 Come, Holy Spirit, now descend!
  Most blessed gift which God can send;
  Thou Fire of love, and Fount of life!
  Consume our sins, and calm our strife.

3 With patience firm and purpose high,
  The weakness of our flesh supply;
  Kindle our senses from above,
  And make our hearts o'erflow with love.

4 Far from us drive the foe we dread,
  And grant us thy true peace instead;
  So shall we not, with thee to guide,
  Turn from the paths of life aside.

Gregory the Great (550—604).

No. 41.   TRURO. L. M.

CHARLES BURNEY (1726—1814).

1 Come, let us tune our loftiest song,
    And raise to Christ our joyful strain;
  Worship and thanks to him belong,
    Who reigns, and shall forever reign.

2 His sovereign power our bodies made;
    Our souls are his immortal breath;
  And when his creatures sinned, he bled,
    To save us from eternal death.

3 Burn every breast with Jesus' love;
    Bound every heart with rapturous joy;
  And saints on earth, with saints above,
    Your voices in his praise employ.

4 Extol the Lamb with loftiest song,
    Ascend for him our cheerful strain;
  Worship and thanks to him belong,
    Who reigns, and shall forever reign.

ROBERT A. WEST.

No. 42. VAN METER. L. M. Double.

F. Mendelssohn (1809 — 1847).

Music on opposite page.

1 He leadeth me! O blessed thought!
   O words with heavenly comfort fraught!
   Whate'er I do, where'er I be,
   Still 't is God's hand that leadeth me.
   He leadeth me, he leadeth me,
   By his own hand he leadeth me:
   ‖: His faithful follower I would be,
   For by his hand he leadeth me.:‖

2 Sometimes 'mid scenes of deepest gloom,
   Sometimes where Eden's bowers bloom,
   By waters still, o'er troubled sea,—
   Still 't is his hand that leadeth me!

3 Lord, I would clasp thy hand in mine,
   Nor ever murmur nor repine,
   Content, whatever lot I see,
   Since 't is my God that leadeth me!

4 And when my task on earth is done,
   When, by thy grace, the victory's won,
   E'en death's cold wave I will not flee,
   Since God through Jordan leadeth me.

   Rev. J. H. GILMORE, 1834.

1 My Lord, how full of sweet content,
   I pass my years of banishment!
   Where'er I dwell, I dwell with thee,
   In heaven, in earth, or on the sea.
   To me remains nor place nor time:
   My country is in every clime:
   ‖: I can be calm and free from care
   On any shore, since God is there.:‖

2 While place we seek, or place we shun,
   The soul finds happiness in none;
   But with a God to guide our way,
   'T is equal joy, to go or stay.
   Could I be cast where thou art not,
   That were indeed a dreadful lot;
   ‖: But regions none remote I call,
   Secure of finding God in all.:‖

   Mad. J. M. B. DE LA MOTTE GUYON, tr. by WM. COWPER.

Music on opposite page.

1 Faith of our fathers! living still
   In spite of dungeon, fire, and sword:
O how our hearts beat high with joy
   Whene'er we hear that glorious word:
Faith of our fathers! holy faith!
We will be true to thee till death!

2 Our fathers, chained in prisons dark,
   Were still in heart and conscience free:
How sweet would be their children's fate,
   If they, like them, could die for thee!
Faith of our fathers! holy faith!
We will be true to thee till death!

3 Faith of our fathers! we will love
   Both friend and foe in all our strife:
And preach thee, too, as love knows how,
   By kindly words and virtuous life:
Faith of our fathers! holy faith!
We will be true to thee till death!

                   FREDERICK W. FABER (1815—1863).

1 When time seems short and death is near,
And I am pressed by doubt and fear,
And sins, an overflowing tide,
Assail my peace on every side,
This thought my refuge still shall be,
I know the Saviour died for me.

2 His name is Jesus, and he died,
For guilty sinners crucified;
Content to die that he might win
Their ransom from the death of sin:
No sinner worse than I can be,
Therefore I know he died for me.

3 If grace were bought, I could not buy;
If grace were coined, no wealth have I;
By grace alone I draw my breath,
Held up from everlasting death;
Yet, since I know his grace is free,
I know the Saviour died for me.

                   Rev. GEORGE W. BETHUNE, D. D. (1805—1862).

No. 45.   WESLEY. L. M.

L. V. BEETHOVEN (1770—1827).

1 Just as I am, without one plea,
  But that thy blood was shed for me,
  And that thou bidd'st me come to thee,
  O Lamb of God, I come! I come!

2 Just as I am — poor, wretched, blind;
  Sight, riches, healing of the mind,
  Yea, all I need in thee to find,
  O Lamb of God, I come! I come!

3 Just as I am — thou wilt receive,
  Wilt welcome, pardon, cleanse, relieve;
  Because thy promise I believe,
  O Lamb of God, I come! I come!

4 Just as I am,— thy love unknown
  Hath broken every barrier down;
  Now, to be thine, yea, thine alone,
  O Lamb of God, I come! I come!

CHARLOTTE ELLIOTT (1789—1871).

1 Father of heaven, whose love profound
  A ransom for our souls hath found,
  Before thy throne we sinners bend;
  To us thy pardoning love extend.

2 Almighty Son, incarnate Word,
  Our Prophet, Priest, Redeemer, Lord,
  Before thy throne, we sinners bend;
  To us thy saving grace extend.

3 Eternal Spirit, by whose breath
  The soul is raised from sin and death,
  Before thy throne we sinners bend;
  To us thy quickening power extend.

4 Jehovah! Father, Spirit, Son!
  Mysterious Godhead! Three in One!
  Before thy throne we sinners bend;
  Grace, pardon, life, to us extend.

JOHN COOPER, 1818.

No. 46.   DENNIS. S. M.

J. G. Naegeli (1768 – 1836).

1 If, or a quiet sea,
   Toward heaven we calmly sail,
With grateful hearts, O God, to thee,
   We'll own the favoring gale.

2 But should the surges rise,
   And rest delay to come,
Blest be the tempest, kind the storm,
   Which drives us nearer home.

3 Soon shall our doubts and fears
   All yield to thy control;
Thy tender mercies shall illume
   The midnight of the soul.

4 Teach us, in every state,
   To make thy will our own;
And when the joys of sense depart,
   To live by faith alone.

Rev. Augustus M. Toplady (1740 – 1778).

No. 47.   DIADEMATA. S. M. Double.

Sir G. J. Elvey (1816—).

1 Crown him with many crowns,
   The Lamb upon his throne;
 Hark, how the heavenly anthem drowns
   All music but its own!
 Awake, my soul, and sing,
   Of him who died for thee,
 And hail him as thy matchless King
   Through all eternity.

2 Crown him the Lord of love!
   Behold his hands and side,—
 Rich wounds, yet visible above,
   In beauty glorified;
 No angel in the sky
   Can fully bear that sight,
 But downward bends his burning eye
   At mysteries so great.

3 Crown him the Lord of peace!
   Whose power a scepter sways
 From pole to pole, that wars may cease,
   And all be prayer and praise:
 His reign shall know no end,
   And round his piercéd feet
 Fair flowers of paradise extend,
   Their fragrance ever sweet.

4 Crown him the Lord of years,
   The Potentate of time,
 Creator of the rolling spheres,
   Ineffably sublime!
 All hail! Redeemer, hail!
   For thou hast died for me;
 Thy praise shall never, never fail
   Throughout eternity.

Matthew Bridges (1800—1852).

No. 48.   HOPKINS. S. M. Double.
                                         HENRY SCHWING, 1825.

1 I was a wandering sheep,
    I did not love the fold;
  I did not love my Shepherd's voice,
    I would not be controlled;
  I was a wayward child,
    I did not love my home,
  I did not love my Father's voice,
    I loved afar to roam.

2 The Shepherd sought his sheep,
    The Father sought his child;
  He followed me o'er vale and hill,
    O'er deserts waste and wild;
  He found me nigh to death,
    Famished, and faint, and lone;
  He bound me with the bands of love,
    He saved the wandering one.

3 Jesus my Shepherd is:
    'T was he that loved my soul,
  'T was he that washed me in his blood,
    'T was he that made me whole:
  'T was he that sought the lost,
    That found the wandering sheep;
  'T was he that brought me to the fold,
    'T was he that still doth keep.

4 No more a wandering sheep,
    I love to be controlled;
  I love my tender Shepherd's voice,
    I love the peaceful fold;
  No more a wayward child,
    I seek no more to roam;
  I love my heavenly Father's voice,
    I love, I love his home!
                Rev. HORATIUS BONAR, D. D. (1808—).

No. 49.   MORNINGTON. S. M.

Earl Mornington (1720—1781).

1 Jesus, my Truth, my Way,
   My sure, unerring Light,
  On thee my feeble steps I stay,
   Which thou wilt guide aright.

2 My Wisdom and my Guide,
   My Counselor thou art:
  O never let me leave thy side,
   Or from thy paths depart.

3 O make me all like thee,
   Before I hence remove;
  Settle, confirm, and 'stablish me,
   And build me up in love.

4 Let me thy witness live,
   When sin is all destroyed;
  And then my spotless soul receive,
   And take me home to God.

Rev. Charles Wesley (1708—1788).

No. 50.   NAILLE. S. M.

L. v. BEETHOVEN (1770—1827).

1 It is not death to die,—
   To leave this weary road,
And, 'mid the brotherhood on high,
   To be at home with God.

2 It is not death to close
   The eye long dimmed by tears,
And wake, in glorious repose
   To spend eternal years.

3 It is not death to bear
   The wrench that sets us free
From dungeon chain, to breathe the air
   Of boundless liberty.

4 It is not death to fling
   Aside this sinful dust,
And rise, on strong exulting wing,
   To live among the just.

5 Jesus, thou Prince of life,
   Thy chosen cannot die!
Like thee, they conquer in the strife,
   To reign with thee on high.

ABRAHAM H. C. MALAN (1787—1864), tr. by G. W. BETHUNE.

No. 51.   SELVIN. S. M.

GERMAN.

1 How beauteous are their feet
  Who stand on Zion's hill,
 ‖:Who bring salvation on their tongues,
  And words of peace reveal !:‖

2 How charming is their voice,
  How sweet the tidings are !
 ‖:"Zion, behold thy Saviour King;
  He reigns and triumphs here.":‖

3 How happy are our ears,
  That hear the joyful sound,
 ‖:Which kings and prophets waited for,
  And sought, but never found !:‖

4 How blessed are our eyes,
  That see this heavenly light !
 ‖:Prophets and kings desired it long,
  But died without the sight.:‖

5 The watchmen join their voice,
  The tuneful notes employ;
 ‖:Jerusalem breaks forth in songs,
  And deserts learn the joy.:‖

6 The Lord makes bare his arm
  Through all the earth abroad;
 ‖:Let every nation now behold
  Their Saviour and their God.:‖

Rev. ISAAC WATTS, D. D. (1674—1748).

No. 52. SHIRLAND. S. M.

S. Stanley (1767—1822).

1 Awake, and sing the song
    Of Moses and the Lamb;
  Wake, every heart and every tongue,
    To praise the Saviour's name.

2 Sing on your heavenly way,
    Ye ransomed sinners, sing;
  Sing on, rejoicing every day
    In Christ, the eternal King.

3 Soon shall we hear him say,
    "Ye blessed children, come!"
  Soon will he call us hence away,
    To our eternal home.

4 There shall each raptured tongue
    His endless praise proclaim;
  And sweeter voices tune the song
    Of Moses and the Lamb.

Rev. William Hammond (1719—1783), alt.

No. 53.   SILVER STREET.   S. M.

Isaac Smith (—1800).

1 Come, sound his praise abroad,
   And hymns of glory sing:
Jehovah is the sovereign God,
   The universal King.

2 He formed the deeps unknown;
   He gave the seas their bound;
The watery worlds are all his own,
   And all the solid ground.

3 Come, worship at his throne,
   Come, bow before the Lord;
We are his works, and not our own;
   He formed us by his word.

4 To-day attend his voice,
   Nor dare provoke his rod;
Come, like the people of his choice,
   And own your gracious God.

Rev. Isaac Watts, D. D. (1674—1748).

No. 54. ST. THOMAS. S. M.

G. F. HANDEL. (1685 — 1759).

1 Had I the gift of tongues,
   Great God, without thy grace,
   My loudest words, my loftiest songs,
   Would be but sounding brass.

2 Though thou shouldst give me skill
   Each mystery to explain,
   Without a heart to do thy will,
   My knowledge would be vain.

3 Had I such faith in God
   As mountains to remove,
   No faith could work effectual good,
   That did not work by love.

4 Grant, then, this one request,
   Whatever be denied,—
   That love divine may rule my breast,
   And all my actions guide.

Rev. SAMUEL STENNETT, D. D.(1721—1795). Alt.

No. 55.   SHELLY. S. M.

L. Spohr (1784—1859).

1 Behold the throne of grace;
   The promise calls us near;
 There Jesus shows a smiling face,
   And waits to answer prayer.

2 My soul, ask what thou wilt,
   Thou canst not be too bold;
 Since his own blood for thee he spilt,
   What else can he withhold?

3 Thine image, Lord, bestow,
   Thy presence and thy love,
 That we may serve thee here below,
   And reign with thee above.

4 Teach us to live by faith,
   Conform our wills to thine;
 Let us victorious be in death,
   And then in glory shine.

Rev. John Newton (1725—1807).

No. 56.   BARTLETT. 7s.

F. T. BARRINGTON.

1 Hark, my soul! it is the Lord;
   'T is thy Saviour,— hear his word:
   Jesus speaks, he speaks to thee:
   "Say, poor sinner, lov'st thou me?"

2 "I delivered thee when bound,
   And, when bleeding, healed thy wound;
   Sought thee wandering, set thee right,
   Turned thy darkness into light.

3 "Thou shalt see my glory soon,
   When the work of faith is done;
   Partner of my throne shalt be;
   Say, poor sinner, lov'st thou me?"

4 Lord, it is my chief complaint
   That my love is weak and faint,
   Yet I love thee and adore:
   O for grace to love thee more!

WILLIAM COWPER (1731—1800).

No. 57. BENNETT. 7s Double.

J. BLUMENTHAL (1829—).

1 Jesus, Lover of my soul,
   Let me to thy bosom fly,
While the nearer waters roll,
   While the tempest still is high!
Hide me, O my Saviour, hide,
   Till the storm of life is past;
Safe into the haven guide,
   O receive my soul at last!

2 Other refuge have I none;
   Hangs my helpless soul on thee:
Leave, O leave me not alone,
   Still support and comfort me:
All my trust on thee is stayed,
   All my help from thee I bring;
Cover my defenseless head
   With the shadow of thy wing!

3 Thou, O Christ, art all I want;
   More than all in thee I find;
Raise the fallen, cheer the faint,
   Heal the sick, and lead the blind.
Just and holy is thy name,
   I am all unrighteousness;
False and full of sin I am,
   Thou art full of truth and grace.

4 Plenteous grace with thee is found,
   Grace to cover all my sin;
Let the healing streams abound;
   Make and keep me pure within.
Thou of life the fountain art,
   Freely let me take of thee;
Spring thou up within my heart,
   Rise to all eternity.

Rev. CHARLES WESLEY (1708—1788).

No. 58.   EWING.   7s, 6 lines.
A. EWING (1830—).

1 Jerusalem the golden,
    With milk and honey blest,
  Beneath thy contemplation
    Sink heart and voice oppressed:
  I know not, O I know not
    What social joys are there;
  What radiancy of glory,
    What light beyond compare.

2 They stand, those halls of Zion,
    All jubilant with song,
  And bright with many an angel,
    And all the martyr throng:
  The Prince is ever in them,
    The daylight is serene;
  The pastures of the blessed
    Are decked in glorious sheen.

3 There is the throne of David;
    And there, from care released,
  The song of them that triumph,
    The shout of them that feast;
  And they who, with their Leader,
    Have conquered in the fight,
  Forever and forever
    Are clad in robes of white.

4 O sweet and blessed country,
    The home of God's elect!
  O sweet and blessed country
    That eager hearts expect!
  Jesus, in mercy bring us
    To that dear land of rest;
  Who art, with God the Father,
    And Spirit, ever blest.

BERNARD OF CLUNY (1122) Tr. by J. M. NEALE.

No. 59. FISHER. 7s, 6 lines.

Miss ELLA M. GUYTON (1871–).
Composed for this work

1 As with gladness men of old
   Did the guiding star behold;
   As with joy they hailed its light,
   Leading onward, beaming bright;
   So, most gracious Lord, may we
   Evermore be led to thee.

2 As with joyful steps they sped
   To that lowly manger-bed,
   There to bend the knee before
   Him whom heaven and earth adore;
   So may we with willing feet
   Ever seek the mercy-seat.

3 As they offered gifts most rare
   At that manger rude and bare;
   So may we with holy joy,
   Pure, and free from sin's alloy,
   All our costliest treasures bring,
   Christ, to thee, our heavenly King.

4 Holy Jesus, every day
   Keep us in the narrow way;
   And, when earthly things are past,
   Bring our ransomed souls at last
   Where they need no star to guide,
   Where no clouds thy glory hide.

WILLIAM C. DIX (1837–).

No. 60. HORTON. 7s.

X. S. v. WARTENSEE (1789—).

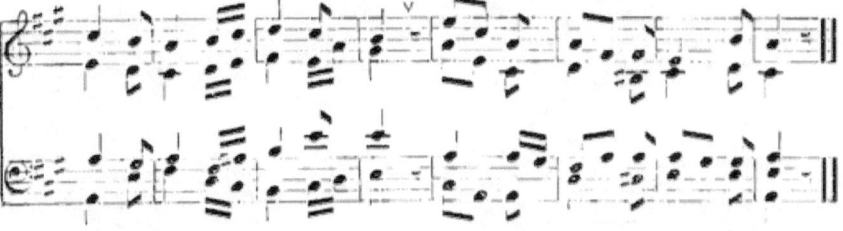

1 Thine forever! — God of love,
   Hear us from thy throne above;
   Thine forever may we be,
   Here and in eternity.

2 Thine forever! — Lord of life,
   Shield us through our earthly strife;
   Thou, the Life, the Truth, the Way,
   Guide us to the realms of day.

3 Thine forever! — Saviour, keep
   These thy frail and trembling sheep:
   Safe alone beneath thy care,
   Let us all thy goodness share.

4 Thine forever! — thou our Guide,
   All our wants by thee supplied,
   All our sins by thee forgiven,
   Lead us, Lord, from earth to heaven.
        Mrs. Mary F. Maude, 1848.

1 Glory be to God on high,
   God, whose glory fills the sky!
   Peace on earth to man forgiven,
   Man, the well-beloved of Heaven.

2 Sovereign Father, heavenly King,
   Thee we now presume to sing;
   Thee with thankful hearts we prove
   God of power, and God of love.

3 Christ our Lord and God we own,
   Christ, the Father's only Son,
   Lamb of God for sinners slain,
   Saviour of offending men.

4 Bow thine ear, in mercy bow,
   Hear, the world's atonement, thou!
   Jesus, in thy name we pray,
   Take, O take our sins away.
        Rev. Charles Wesley (1708—1788).

No. 61. GOUCHER. 7s, 6 lines.

F. MENDELSSOHN (1809 — 1847).

1 As with gladness men of old
  Did the guiding star behold;
  As with joy they hailed its light,
  Leading onward, beaming bright;
  So, most gracious Lord, may we
  Evermore be led to thee.

2 As with joyful steps they sped
  To that lowly manger-bed,
  There to bend the knee before
  Him whom heaven and earth adore;
  So may we with willing feet
  Ever seek the mercy-seat.

3 As they offered gifts most rare
  At that manger rude and bear;
  So may we with holy joy,
  Pure, and free from sin's alloy,
  All our costliest treasures bring,
  Christ, to thee, our heavenly King.

4 Holy Jesus, every day
  Keep us in the narrow way;
  And, when earthly things are past,
  Bring our ransomed souls at last
  Where they need no star to guide,
  Where no clouds thy glory hide.

WILLIAM C. DIX.

No. 62.   HENDON. 7s.

Rev. A. H. C. Malan (1787—1864).

1 They who seek the throne of grace,
  Find that throne in every place;
  If we live a life of prayer,
  ‖:God is present every-where.:‖

2 In our sickness or our health,
  In our want or in our wealth,
  If we look to God in prayer,
  God is present every-where.

3 When our earthly comforts fail,
  When the foes of life prevail,
  'T is the time for earnest prayer;
  God is present every-where.

4 Then, my soul, in every strait
  To Thy Father come and wait;
  He will answer every prayer;
  God is present every-where.

OLIVER HOLDEN, alt (1765—1844).

No. 63.   LITANY HYMN.   7s, 8 lines.

1 Saviour, when, in dust, to thee
Low we bend th' adoring knee;
When, repentant, to the skies
Scarce we lift our weeping eyes;
O by all the pains and woe
Suffered once for man below,
Bending from thy throne on high,
Hear our solemn litany!

2 By thy helpless infant years;
By thy life of want and tears;
By thy days of sore distress,
In the savage wilderness;
By the dread mysterious hour
Of the insulting tempter's power;
Turn, O turn a favoring eye,
Hear our solemn litany!

3 By the sacred griefs that wept
O'er the grave where Lazarus slept;
By the boding tears that flowed
Over Salem's loved abode;
By the anguished sigh that told
Treachery lurked within thy fold;
From thy seat above the sky,
Hear our solemn litany!

4 By thine hour of dire despair;
By thine agony of prayer;
By the cross, the nail, the thorn,
Piercing spear, and torturing scorn;
By the gloom that veiled the skies
O'er the dreadful sacrifice;
Listen to our humble cry,
Hear our solemn litany!

5 By thy deep, expiring groan;
By the sad sepulchral stone;
By the vault whose dark abode
Held in vain the rising God;
O from earth to heaven restored,
Mighty, re-ascended Lord,
Listen, listen to the cry
Of our solemn litany!

Sir ROBERT GRANT (1785—1838).

No. 64.   NÜREMBERG.   7s.

J. R. Ahle (1625—1673).

1 Holy Spirit, Truth divine!
  Dawn upon this soul of mine;
  Word of God, and inward Light!
  Wake my spirit, clear my sight.

2 Holy Spirit, Love divine!
  Glow within this heart of mine;
  Kindle every high desire;
  Perish self in thy pure fire!

3 Holy Spirit, Power divine!
  Fill and nerve this will of mine;
  By thee may I strongly live,
  Bravely bear, and nobly strive.

4 Holy Spirit, Right divine!
  King within my conscience reign;
  Be my law, and I shall be
  Firmly bound, forever free.

Rev. Samuel Longfellow (1819—).

No. 65. PLEYEL'S HYMN. 7s.

I. Pleyel (1757 — 1831).

1 Never further than thy cross;
   Never higher than thy feet;
  Here earth's precious things seem dross;
   Here earth's bitter things grow sweet.

2 Here we learn to serve and give,
   And, rejoicing, self deny;
  Here we gather love to live,
   Here we gather faith to die.

3 Pressing onward as we can,
   Still to this our hearts must tend;
  Where our earliest hopes began,
   There our last aspirings end;

4 Till amid the hosts of light,
   We in thee redeemed, complete,
  Through thy cross made pure and white,
   Cast our crowns before thy feet.

Mrs. Elizabeth Charles, 1865.

No. 66.   REPOSE.   7s, 6 lines.

F. Kücken (1810 —).

1 Chief of sinners though I be,
  Jesus shed his blood for me;
  Died that I might live on high,
  Died that I might never die;
  As the branch is to the vine,
  I am his and he is mine.

2 O the height of Jesus' love!
  Higher than the heavens above,
  Deeper than the depths of sea,
  Lasting as eternity;
  Love that found me,—wondrous thought!
  Found me when I sought him not!

3 Chief of sinners though I be,
  Christ is all in all to me;
  All my wants to him are known,
  All my sorrows are his own;
  Safe with him from earthly strife,
  He sustains the hidden life.

McComb.

No. 67. WORTHINGTON. 8s & 7s.

C. M. v. Weber (1786—1826).

1 There's a wideness in God's mercy,
   Like the wideness of the sea:
   There's a kindness in his justice,
   Which is more than liberty.

2 There is welcome for the sinner,
   And more graces for the good;
   There is mercy with the Saviour;
   There is healing in his blood.

3 For the love of God is broader
   Than the measure of man's mind;
   And the heart of the Eternal
   Is most wonderfully kind.

4 If our love were but more simple,
   We should take him at his word;
   And our lives would be all sunshine
   In the sweetness of our Lord.

Rev. Frederick W. Faber (1815—1863).

No. 68.   AUSTRIA.   8s & 7s, Double.
J. Haydn (1732—1809).

1 Glorious things of thee are spoken,
   Zion, city of our God;
 He, whose word cannot be broken,
   Formed thee for his own abode;
 On the Rock of ages founded,
   What can shake thy sure repose?
 With salvation's walls surrounded,
   Thou mayst smile at all thy foes.

2 See, the streams of living waters,
   Springing from eternal love,
 Still supply thy sons and daughters,
   And all fear of want remove:

Who can faint while such a river
   Ever flows our thirst to assuage?
Grace, which, like the Lord the giver,
   Never fails from age to age.

3 Round each habitation hovering,
   See the cloud and fire appear,
 For a glory and a covering,
   Showing that the Lord is near!
 He who gives us daily manna,
   He who listens when we cry,
 Let him hear the loud hosanna
   Rising to his throne on high.

Rev. John Newton (1725—1807).

No. 69.   ANGELUS.   8s & 7s, 6 lines.

German Choral.

1 I will praise thee, Sun of Glory!
   For thy beams have gladness brought;
  I will praise thee, will adore thee,
   For the light I vainly sought;
  Will praise thee that thy words so blest,
   Spake my sin-sick soul to rest.

2 In thy footsteps now uphold me,
   That I stumble not nor stray,
  When the narrow way is told me,
   Never let me lingering stay.
  But come, my weary soul to cheer,
   Shine, eternal Sunbeam here!

3 Be my heart more warmly glowing,
   Sweet and calm the tears I shed;
  And its love, its ardor showing,
   Let my spirit onward tread
  Still near to thee, and nearer still,
   Draw this heart, this mind, this will.

4 I will love, in joy and sorrow!
   Crowning joy! will love thee well!
  I will love, to-day, to-morrow,
   While I in this body dwell.
  Oh! I will love thee, Light Divine,
   Till I die, and find thee mine!

JOHANN SCHEFFLER (ANGELUS).

No. 70.   AUTUMN. 8s & 7s, Double.

1 Sing with all the sons of glory,
    Sing the resurrection song!
  Death and sorrow, earth's dark story,
    To the former days belong;
  All around the clouds are breaking,
    Soon the storms of time shall cease,
  In God's likeness, man awaking,
    Knows the everlasting peace.

2 O what glory, far exceeding
    All that eye has yet perceived!
  Holiest hearts for ages pleading,
    Never that full joy conceived.
  God has promised, Christ prepares it,
    There on high our welcome waits;
  Every humble spirit shares it,
    Christ has passed the eternal gates.

3 Life eternal! heaven rejoices,
    Jesus lives who once was dead;
  Join, O man, the deathless voices,
    Child of God, lift up thy head!
  Patriarchs from the distant ages,
    Saints all longing for their heaven,
  Prophets, psalmists, seers and sages,
    All await the glory given.

4 Life eternal! O what wonders
    Crowd on faith; what joy unknown,
  When, amidst earth's closing thunders,
    Saints shall stand before the throne!
  O to enter that bright portal,
    See that glowing firmament,
  Know, with thee, O God immortal,
    "Jesus Christ whom thou hast sent."
      Rev. WILLIAM J. IRONS, D. D. (1812—).

No. 71. DULCETTA. 8s, 7s.
BEETHOVEN (1770—1827).

1 Laboring and heavy laden,
  Wanting help in time of need,
  Fainting by the way from hunger,
  "Bread of life!" on thee we feed.

2 Thirsting for the springs of waters
  That, by love's eternal law,
  From the stricken Rock are flowing,
  "Well of life!" from thee we draw.

3 In the land of cloud and shadow,
  Where no human eye can see,
  Light to those who sit in darkness,
  "Light of life!" we walk in thee.

4 Thou the grace of life supplying,
  Thou the crown of life wilt give;
  Dead to sin, and daily dying,
  "Life of life!" in thee we live.

Rev. JOHN S. B. MONSELL (1811—1875).

No. 72. JENNIE. 8s, 7s.

H. Schwing. 1825.

1 Praise the Lord! ye heavens, adore him;
  Praise him, angels, in the height;
  Sun and moon, rejoice before him;
  ||: Praise him, all ye stars of light. :||

2 Praise the Lord, for he hath spoken;
  Worlds his mighty voice obeyed;
  Laws which never shall be broken,
  For their guidance he hath made.

3 Praise the Lord, for he is glorious;
  Never shall his promise fail;
  God hath made his saints victorious;
  Sin and death shall not prevail.

4 Praise the God of our salvation;
  Hosts on high, his power proclaim;
  Heaven and earth, and all creation,
  Laud and magnify his name.

Rev. JOHN KEMPTHORNE (1775—1838).

No. 73. RATHBUN. 8s & 7s.

I. CONKEY (1815—1867).

1 God is love; his mercy brightens
　All the path in which we rove;
　Bliss he wakes and woe he lightens;
　　God is wisdom, God is love.

2 Chance and change are busy ever;
　Man decays, and ages move;
　But his mercy waneth never;
　　God is wisdom, God is love.

3 E'en the hour that darkest seemeth,
　Will his changeless goodness prove;
　From the gloom his brightness streameth,
　　God is wisdom, God is love.

4 He with earthly cares entwineth
　Hope and comfort from above;
　Every-where his glory shineth;
　　God is wisdom, God is love.

Sir JOHN BOWRING, LL.D. (1792—1872).

No. 74.   SICILIAN HYMN.   8s & 7s.

1 Love divine, all love excelling,
  Joy of heaven, to earth come down!
Fix in us thy humble dwelling;
  All thy faithful mercies crown.
Jesus, thou art all compassion,
  Pure unbounded love thou art;
Visit us with thy salvation;
  Enter every trembling heart.

2 Breathe, O breathe thy loving Spirit
  Into every troubled breast!
Let us all in thee inherit,
  Let us find that second rest.
Take away our bent to sinning;
  Alpha and Omega be;
End of faith, as its beginning,
  Set our hearts at liberty.

3 Come, almighty to deliver,
  Let us all thy life receive;
Suddenly return, and never,
  Never more thy temples leave:
Thee we would be always blessing,
  Serve thee as thy hosts above,
Pray, and praise thee without ceasing,
  Glory in thy perfect love.

4 Finish then thy new creation;
  Pure and spotless let us be;
Let us see thy great salvation,
  Perfectly restored in thee:
Changed from glory into glory,
  Till in heaven we take our place,
Till we cast our crowns before thee,
  Lost in wonder, love, and praise.

REV. CHARLES WESLEY (1708—1788).

No. 75. WILCOX. 8s & 7s, Double.

G. A. Herrmann.
Composed for this work.

1 Love divine, all love excelling,
    Joy of heaven, to earth come down!
Fix in us thy humble dwelling;
    All thy faithful mercies crown.
Jesus, thou art all compassion,
    Pure unbounded love thou art;
Visit us with thy salvation;
    Enter every trembling heart.

2 Breathe, O breathe thy loving Spirit
    Into every troubled breast!
Let us all in thee inherit,
    Let us find that second rest.
Take away our bent to sinning;
    Alpha and Omega be;
End of faith, as its beginning,
    Set our hearts at liberty.

3 Come, almighty to deliver,
    Let us all thy life receive;
Suddenly return, and never,
    Never more thy temples leave:
Thee we would be always blessing,
    Serve thee as thy hosts above,
Pray, and praise thee without ceasing,
    Glory in thy perfect love.

4 Finish then thy new creation;
    Pure and spotless let us be;
Let us see thy great salvation,
    Perfectly restored in thee:
Changed from glory into glory,
    Till in heaven we take our place,
Till we cast our crowns before thee,
    Lost in wonder, love, and praise.
                  CHARLES WESLEY.

No. 76.　　　　WILMOT.　8s & 7s.

C. M. v. Weber (1786—1826).

1 Hark! what mean those holy voices,
　　Sweetly sounding through the skies?
　Lo! the angelic host rejoices;
　　Heavenly hallelujahs rise.

2 Listen to the wondrous story,
　　Which they chant in hymns of joy:
　"Glory in the highest, glory,
　　Glory be to God most high!

3 "Peace on earth, good-will from heaven,
　　Reaching far as man is found;
　Souls redeemed and sins forgiven!
　　Loud our golden harps shall sound.

4 "Christ is born, the great Anointed;
　　Heaven and earth his praises sing;
　O receive whom God appointed,
　　For your Prophet, Priest, and King.

5 "Hasten, mortals, to adore him:
　　Learn his name, and taste his joy;
　Till in heaven ye sing before him,
　　'Glory be to God most high!'"

Rev John Cawood (1775—1852).

No. 77.　　　　　AMERICA.　6s & 4s.

H. Carey (1685 — 1743).

1　My country! 't is of thee,
　　Sweet land of liberty,
　　　Of thee I sing:
　　Land where my fathers died!
　　Land of the pilgrims' pride!
　　From every mountain side
　　　Let freedom ring!

2　My native country, thee,
　　Land of the noble, free,
　　　Thy name I love;
　　I love thy rocks and rills,
　　Thy woods and templed hills:
　　My heart with rapture thrills
　　　Like that above.

3　Let music swell the breeze,
　　And ring from all the trees
　　　Sweet freedom's song;
　　Let mortal tongues awake;
　　Let all that breathe partake;
　　Let rocks their silence break,
　　　The sound prolong.

4　Our fathers' God! to thee,
　　Author of liberty,
　　　To thee we sing;
　　Long may our land be bright
　　With freedom's holy light;
　　Protect us by thy might,
　　　Great God, our King!

Rev. Samuel F. Smith, D. D. (1808 —).

No. 78.   AMERICA.   6s & 4s.

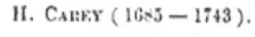
H. Carey (1685—1743).

1 Thou, whose almighty word
    Chaos and darkness heard,
        And took their flight;
    Hear us, we humbly pray,
    And where the gospel day
    Sheds not its glorious ray,
        "Let there be light."

2 Thou, who didst come to bring
    On thy redeeming wing,
        Healing and sight,
    Health to the sick in mind,
    Sight to the inly blind;
    O now, to all mankind,
        "Let there be light."

3 Spirit of truth and love,
    Life-giving, holy Dove,
        Speed forth thy flight;
    Move o'er the waters' face
    By thine almighty grace;
    And in earth's darkest place,
        "Let there be light."

4 Blessed and holy Three,
    Glorious Trinity,
        Wisdom, Love, Might;
    Boundless as ocean's tide
    Rolling in fullest pride,
    O'er the world far and wide,
        "Let there be light."

Rev. John Marriott (1780—1825).

No. 79. AMSTERDAM. 7s & 6s.

JAMES NARES (1715—1783).

1 Rise, my soul, and stretch thy wings,
   Thy better portion trace;
  Rise from transitory things
   Toward heaven, thy native place:
  Sun, and moon, and stars decay;
   Time shall soon this earth remove;
  Rise, my soul, and haste away
   To seats prepared above.

2 Rivers to the ocean run,
   Nor stay in all their course;
  Fire ascending seeks the sun;
   Both speed them to their source:

So a soul that's born of God,
 Pants to view his glorious face;
Upward tends to his abode,
 To rest in his embrace.

3 Cease, ye pilgrims, cease to mourn,
   Press onward to the prize;
  Soon our Saviour will return
   Triumphant in the skies:
  There we'll join the heavenly train,
   Welcomed to partake the bliss;
  Fly from sorrow, care, and pain,
   To realms of endless peace.

REV. ROBERT SEAGRAVE, 1693.

NO. 80. ARIEL. C. P. M.

L. Mason (1792—1872.)

1 O could I speak the matchless worth,
  O could I sound the glories forth,
    Which in my Saviour shine.
  I'd soar and touch the heavenly strings,
  And vie with Gabriel while he sings
    ‖: In notes almost divine. :‖

2 I'd sing the precious blood he spilt,
  My ransom from the dreadful guilt
    Of sin, and wrath divine;
  I'd sing his glorious righteousness,
  In which all-perfect, heavenly dress
    ‖: My soul shall ever shine. :‖

3 I'd sing the characters he bears,
  And all the forms of love he wears,
    Exalted on his throne;
  In loftiest songs of sweetest praise,
  I would to everlasting days
    ‖: Make all his glories known. :‖

4 Well, the delightful day will come
  When my dear Lord will bring me home,
    And I shall see his face;
  Then with my Saviour, Brother, Friend,
  A blest eternity I'll spend,
    ‖: Triumphant in his grace. :‖

Samuel Medley (1738—1799).

No. 81.   FORTRESS.   8s, 7s & 6s.

MARTIN LUTHER (1483—1546).

1 A mighty fortress is our God,
   A bulwark never failing:
 Our Helper he, amid the flood
   Of mortal ills prevailing.
 For still our ancient foe
 Doth seek to work us woe;
   His craft and power are great,
   And, armed with cruel hate,
 On earth is not his equal.

2 Did we in our own strength confide,
   Our striving would be losing;
 Were not the right man on our side,
   The man of God's own choosing.
 Dost ask who that may be?
 Christ Jesus, it is he;
   Lord Sabaoth is his name,
   From age to age the same,
 And he must win the battle.

3 That word above all earthly powers —
   No thanks to them — abideth;
 The Spirit and the gifts are ours
   Through him who with us sideth.
 Let goods and kindred go,
 This mortal life also:
   The body they may kill:
   God's truth abideth still,
 His kingdom is forever.

MARTIN LUTHER, tr. by F. H. HEDGE.

No. 82. IN THE HOUR OF TRIAL. 6s & 5s.

UNKNOWN.

1 In the hour of trial,
  Jesus, plead for me;
Lest by base denial
  I depart from thee.
When thou seest me waver,
  With a look recall,
Nor for fear or favor
  Suffer me to fall.

2 Should thy mercy send me
  Sorrow, toil and woe;
Or should pain attend me
  On my path below;
Grant that I may never
  Fail thy hand to see;
Grant that I may ever
  Cast my care on thee.

3 When my last hour cometh
  Fraught with strife, and pain,
When my dust returneth
  To the dust again.
On thy truth relying
  Through that mortal strife,
Jesus take me dying
  To eternal life.

No. 83. MARY. 10s, 4 lines.

Arr. from E. MEYER-HELMUND.

1 As pants the wearied hart for cooling springs,
   That sinks exhausted in the summer's chase,
 So pants my soul for thee, great King of kings,
   So thirsts to reach thy sacred dwelling place.

2 Lord, thy sure mercies ever in my sight,
   My heart shall gladden through the tedious day;
 And 'midst the dark and gloomy shades of night,
   To thee, my God, I'll tune the grateful lay.

3 Why faint, my soul? why doubt Jehovah's aid?
   Thy God the God of mercy still shall prove;
 Within his courts thy thanks shall yet be paid:
   Unquestion'd be his faithfulness and love.

No. 84.   EVENTIDE. 10s.

W. H. Monk (1861—).

Music on opposite page.

1 Saviour, again to thy dear name we raise,
   With one accord, our parting hymn of praise;
   We stand to bless thee ere our worship cease,
   Then lowly kneeling, wait thy word of peace.

2 Grant us thy peace upon our homeward way;
   With thee began, with thee shall end the day;
   Guard thou the lips from sin, the hearts from shame,
   That in this house have called upon thy name.

3 Grant us thy peace, Lord, through the coming night,
   Turn thou for us its darkness into light;
   From harm and danger keep thy children free,
   For dark and light are both alike to thee.

4 Grant us thy peace throughout our earthly life,
   Our balm in sorrow, and our stay in strife;
   Then, when thy voice shall bid our conflict cease,
   Call us, O Lord, to thine eternal peace.

                                   JOHN ELLERTON.

No. 85.   CHANT.

No. 86.   GREENVILLE.   8s, 7s & 4s.

J. J. Rousseau (1712—1786).

1 Christ is coming! let creation
  Bid her groans and travail cease;
  Let the glorious proclamation
  Hope restore and faith increase;
    : Christ is coming! :
  Come, thou blessed Prince of peace!

2 Earth can now but tell the story
  Of thy bitter cross and pain;
  She shall yet behold thy glory
  When thou comest back to reign;
    : Christ is coming! :
  Let each heart repeat the strain.

3 Long thy exiles have been pining,
  Far from rest, and home, and thee;
  But, in heavenly vesture shining,
  Soon they shall thy glory see;
    : Christ is coming! :
  Haste the joyous jubilee.

4 With that "blessed hope" before us,
  Let no harp remain unstrung;
  Let the mighty advent chorus
  Onward roll from tongue to tongue;
    : Christ is coming! :
  Come, Lord Jesus, quickly come!

Rev. John R. Macduff 1853—.

No. 87.   JEWETT. 6s.
C. M. von Weber (1786—1826).

1 Thy way, not mine, O Lord,
    However dark it be!
  Lead me by thine own hand;
    Choose out the path for me.
  I dare not choose my lot;
    I would not if I might;
  Choose thou for me, my God,
    So shall I walk aright.

2 The kingdom that I seek
    Is thine; so let the way
  That leads to it be thine,
    Else I must surely stray.

  Take thou my cup, and it
    With joy or sorrow fill,
  As best to thee may seem;
    Choose thou my good and ill.

3 Choose thou for me my friends,
    My sickness or my health;
  Choose thou my cares for me,
    My poverty or wealth.
  Not mine, not mine the choice,
    In things or great or small;
  Be thou my guide, my strength,
    My wisdom, and my all.
            Rev. Horatius Bonar, D.D. (1808—).

No. 88.   O HOLY SAVIOUR.   8s, 8s, 8s & 5s.

FLEMMING.

1 O holy Saviour, Friend unseen,
  Since on thine arm thou bidst me lean,
  Help me, throughout life's changing scene,
      By faith to cling to thee!

2 What though the world deceitful prove,
  Our earthly friends and hopes remove,
  With patient, uncomplaining love,
      Still would I cling to thee!

3 Though oft I seem to tread alone
  Life's dreary waste, with thorns o'ergrown,
  Thy voice of love, in gentlest tone,
      Still whispers: "Cling to me!"

4 Though faith and hope are often tried,
  I ask not, need not, aught beside;
  So safe, so calm, so satisfied,
      The soul that clings to thee!

SHIRK.

No. 89. IN THE SILENT MIDNIGHT WATCHES. 8s & 5s.

G. A. HERMANN (1872—).
Composed for this work.

1 In the silent midnight watches,
   List — thy bosom's door!
How it knocketh, knocketh, knocketh,
   Knocketh evermore!
Say not 't is thy pulse's beating,
   'Tis thy heart of sin;
'Tis thy Saviour knocks, and crieth,
   "Rise, and let me in!"

2 Death comes down with reckless footsteps,
   To the hall and hut;
Think you death will tarry knocking,
   When the door is shut?
Jesus waiteth, waiteth, waiteth;
   But the door is fast;
Grieved, away thy Saviour goeth,
   Death breaks in at last.

3 Then 't is time to stand entreating
   Christ to let thee in;
At the gate of heaven beating,
   Wailing for thy sin;
Nay! alas, thou guilty creature!
   Hast thou, then, forgot?
Jesus waited long to know thee,
   Now He knows thee not!

A. CLEVELAND COXE.

No. 90.   ITALIAN HYMN.   6s & 4s.

F. GIARDINI (1716—1796).

1 Rise, glorious Conqueror, rise
   Into thy native skies;
   Assume thy right;
 And where in many a fold
 The clouds are backward rolled,
 Pass through those gates of gold,
   And reign in light!

2 Victor o'er death and hell,
   Cherubic legions swell
   The radiant train:
 Praises all heaven inspire;
 Each angel sweeps his lyre,
 And claps his wings of fire,
   Thou Lamb once slain!

3 Enter, incarnate God!
   No feet but thine have trod
   The serpent down:
 Blow the full trumpets, blow,
 Wider yon portals throw,
 Saviour, triumphant, go,
   And take thy crown!

4 Lion of Judah, hail!
   And let thy name prevail
   From age to age:
 Lord of the rolling years,
 Claim for thine own the spheres,
 For thou hast bought with tears
   Thy heritage.

MATTHEW BRIDGES (1800—1852).

No. 91.   WEBB. 7s & 6s.
G. F. WEBB.

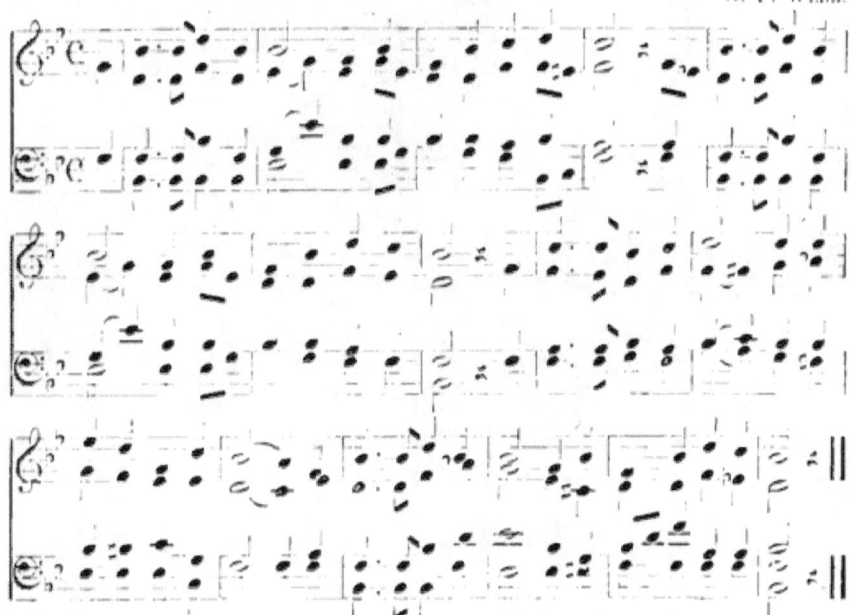

1 Stand up, stand up for Jesus,
   Ye soldiers of the cross;
 Lift high his royal banner,
   It must not suffer loss;
 From victory unto victory
   His army shall he lead,
 Till every foe is vanquished
   And Christ is Lord indeed.

2 Stand up, stand up for Jesus,
   The trumpet call obey;
 Forth to the mighty conflict,
   In this his glorious day;
 "Ye that are men, now serve him,"
   Against unnumbered foes;
 Your courage rise with danger,
   And strength to strength oppose.

3 Stand up, stand up for Jesus,
   Stand in his strength alone;
 The arm of flesh will fail you;
   Ye dare not trust your own;
 Put on the gospel armor,
   Each piece put on with prayer;
 Where duty calls, or danger,
   Be never wanting there.

4 Stand up, stand up for Jesus,
   The strife will not be long;
 This day the noise of battle,
   The next the victor's song;
 To him that overcometh,
   A crown of life shall be;
 He with the King of glory
   Shall reign eternally.

Rev. Geo. Duffield, Jr., D.D., 1848.

No. 92.   LYONS. 10s & 11s.
JOSEPH HAYDN (1732—1819).

1 Ye servants of God, your Master proclaim,
   And publish abroad his wonderful name;
   The name all-victorious of Jesus extol;
   His kingdom is glorious, and rules over all.

2 God ruleth on high, almighty to save;
   And still he is nigh; his presence we have:
   The great congregation his triumph shall sing,
   Ascribing salvation to Jesus, our King.

3 "Salvation to God, who sits on the throne,"
   Let all cry aloud, and honor the Son:
   The praises of Jesus the angels proclaim,
   Fall down on their faces, and worship the Lamb.

4 Then let us adore, and give him his right,
   All glory and power, all wisdom and might,
   All honor and blessing, with angels above,
   And thanks never ceasing for infinite love.

REV. CHARLES WESLEY (1708—1788).

No. 93.   NICEA. 11s, 12s & 10s.

Rev. J. B. DYKES (1823—1876).

1 Holy, holy, holy, Lord God Almighty!
    Early in the morning our song shall rise to thee;
  Holy, holy, holy, merciful and mighty,
    God in Three Persons, blessed Trinity!

2 Holy, holy, holy! all the saints adore thee,
    Casting down their golden crowns around the glassy sea;
  Cherubim and seraphim falling down before thee,
    Which wert, and art, and evermore shalt be.

3 Holy, holy, holy! though the darkness hide thee,
    Though the eye of sinful man thy glory may not see;
  Only thou art holy; there is none beside thee,
    Perfect in power, in love, and purity.

4 Holy, holy, holy, Lord God Almighty!
    All thy works shall praise thy name, in earth, and sky, and sea;
  Holy, holy, holy, merciful and mighty,
    God in Three Persons, blessed Trinity!

(97)   Bishop REGINALD HEBER, D.D. (1783—1826).

No. 94. ONWARD. (CHRISTUS VICTOR.) 6s & 5s.

A. S. Sullivan (1842—).

Music on opposite page.

1 Onward, Christian soldiers!
    Marching as to war,
With the cross of Jesus
    Going on before.
Christ, the royal Master,
    Leads against the foe;
Forward into battle,
    See his banners go!
        Onward, Christian soldiers!
            Marching as to war,
        With the cross of Jesus
            Going on before.

2 At the sign of triumph
    Satan's host doth flee;
On, then, Christian soldiers,
    On to victory!
Hell's foundations quiver
    At the shout of praise;
Brothers, lift your voices,
    Loud your anthems raise.

3 Crowns and thrones may perish,
    Kingdoms rise and wane,
But the Church of Jesus
    Constant will remain;
Gates of hell can never
    'Gainst that Church prevail;
We have Christ's own promise,
    And that cannot fail.

4 Onward, then, ye people!
    Join our happy throng,
Blend with ours your voices
    In the triumph-song;
Glory, laud, and honor
    Unto Christ the King,
This through countless ages
    Men and angels sing.

                Rev. SABINE BARING-GOULD (1834—).

No. 95.　　　　O SACRED HEAD.　　7s & 6s.

K. H. GRAUN (1701—1759).

1　O sacred Head, now wounded,
　　With grief and shame weighed down,
　Now scornfully surrounded
　　With thorns, thine only crown;
　O sacred Head, what glory,
　　What bliss, till now was thine!
　Yet, though despised and gory,
　　I joy to call thee mine.

2　What thou, my Lord, hast suffered
　　Was all for sinners' gain:
　Mine, mine was the transgression,
　　But thine the deadly pain:
　Lo, here I fall, my Saviour!
　　'T is I deserve thy place;
　Look on me with thy favor,
　　Vouchsafe to me thy grace.

3　What language shall I borrow
　　To thank thee, dearest Friend,
　For this, thy dying sorrow,
　　Thy pity without end?
　O make me thine forever;
　　And should I fainting be,
　Lord, let me never, never,
　　Outlive my love to thee.

4　Be near me when I'm dying,
　　O show thy cross to me;
　And, for my succor flying,
　　Come, Lord, and set me free:
　These eyes, new faith receiving,
　　From Jesus shall not move;
　For he who dies believing,
　　Dies safely, through thy love.

BERNARD OF CLAIRVAUX, PAUL GERHARDT.
Tr. by J. W. ALEXANDER (1091—1153).

No. 96.   PAX DEI. 11s & 10s.

Rev. J. B. Dykes (1823 — 1876).

1 Come unto me, when shadows darkly gather,
   When the sad heart is weary and distressed,
  Seeking for comfort from your heavenly Father,
   Come unto me, and I will give you rest.

2 Large are the mansions in thy Father's dwelling,
   Glad are the homes that sorrows never dim;
  Sweet are the harps in holy music swelling,
   Soft are the tones which raise the heavenly hymn.

3 There, like an Eden blossoming in gladness,
   Bloom the fair flowers the earth too rudely pressed;
  Come unto me, all ye who droop in sadness,
   Come unto me, and I will give you rest.

                                    Unknown.

No. 97. ST. PAUL'S.

Rev. J. S. B. Hodges, D. D.
Composed for this work.

1 Wave, wave the Banner,
  Raise the cross on high,
Sing of Jesus' glory,
  Of Christ who deigned to die.
On, on, ye wanderers,
  Homeward wend your way,
Dark may be the evening,
  But brighter far the day.
    Wave, wave, etc.

2 Wave, wave the Banner,
  See! a Cross is nigh,
Jesus on it hangeth,
  Lifted up on high.

Rest, rest, ye pilgrims,
  Rest beneath the Tree,
Hark! He gently calleth,
  Sinners, come to me.
    Wave, wave, etc.

3 Shout, shout, ye victors,
  Ye whose fight is done,
Ye whose toil is over,
  Whose crown of life is won
On, on, ye wanderers,
  Homeward wend your way,
Dark may be the evening,
  But brighter far the day.
    Wave, wave, etc.

(102)

No. 98.   PARADISE.   8s, 6s & 6s.

J. BARNBY (1838—).

1 O paradise! O paradise!
  Who doth not crave for rest?
  Who would not seek the happy land
    Where they that loved are blest;
  Where loyal hearts and true
    Stand ever in the light,
  All rapture through and through,
    In God's most holy sight?

2 O paradise! O paradise!
  The world is growing old;
  Who would not be at rest and free
    Where Love is never cold?

3 O paradise! O paradise!
  'T is weary waiting here;
  I long to be where Jesus is,
    To feel, to see him near.

4 O paradise! O paradise!
  I want to sin no more,
  I want to be as pure on earth
    As on thy spotless shore.

5 O paradise! O paradise!
  I greatly long to see
  The special place my dearest Lord
    In love prepares for me.

Rev. FREDERICK W. FABER, D. D. (1815—1863).

No. 99.   PORTUGUESE HYMN. 11s.

1. How firm a foundation, ye saints of the Lord,
   Is laid for your faith in his excellent word!
   What more can he say, than to you he hath said,
   : To you, who for refuge to Jesus have fled? :

2. "Fear not, I am with thee, O be not dismayed,
   For I am thy God, I will still give thee aid;
   I'll strengthen thee, help thee, and cause thee to stand,
   Upheld by my gracious, omnipotent hand.

3. "When through the deep waters I call thee to go,
   The rivers of sorrow shall not overflow;
   For I will be with thee thy trials to bless,
   And sanctify to thee thy deepest distress.

4. "The soul that on Jesus hath leaned for repose,
   I will not, I will not desert to his foes;
   That soul, though all hell should endeavor to shake,
   I'll never, no never, no never forsake!"

GEORGE KEITH. 1787.

No. 100.   PRAYER.   8s, 8s, 8s & 4s.

Rev. J. B. Dykes (1823—1876).

1 My God, is any hour so sweet,
    From blush of morn to evening star,
  As that which calls me to thy feet,
    The hour of prayer?

2 Blest is that tranquil hour of morn,
    And blest that solemn hour of eve,
  When, on the wings of prayer upborne,
    The world I leave.

3 Then is my strength by thee renewed;
    Then are my sins by thee forgiven;
  Then dost thou cheer my solitude
    With hopes of heaven.

4 No words can tell what sweet relief
    Here for my every want I find;
  What strength for warfare, balm for grief,
    What peace of mind.

5 Hushed is each doubt, gone every fear;
    My spirit seems in heaven to stay;
  And e'en the penitential tear
    Is wiped away.

6 Lord, till I reach that blissful shore,
    No privilege so dear shall be,
  As thus my inmost soul to pour
    In prayer to thee.

CHARLOTTE ELLIOTT (1789—1871).

No. 101. REGENT SQUARE. 8s, 7s & 4s. 6 lines.

HENRY SMART (1812—).

1 O thou God of my salvation,
   My Redeemer from all sin;
  Moved by thy divine compassion,
   Who hast died my heart to win,
    ‖: I will praise thee; :‖
   Where shall I thy praise begin?

2 Though unseen, I love the Saviour;
   He hath brought salvation near;
  Manifests his pardoning favor;
   And when Jesus doth appear,
    ‖: Soul and body :‖
   Shall his glorious image bear.

3 While the angel choirs are crying,
   "Glory to the great I AM."
  I with them will still be vying —
   Glory! glory to the Lamb!
    ‖: O how precious :‖
   Is the sound of Jesus' name!

4 Angels now are hovering round us,
   Unperceived amid the throng;
  Wondering at the love that crowned us,
   Glad to join the holy song:
    ‖: Hallelujah! :‖
   Love and praise to Christ belong!

Rev. THOMAS OLIVERS (1725—1799).

No. 102.   RIGHINI.   6s & 4s.

Z. RIGHINI (1756 — 1812).

1 Come, Holy Ghost, in love,
  Shed on us from above
    Thine own bright ray!
  Divinely good thou art;
  Thy sacred gifts impart
  To gladden each sad heart:
    O come to-day!

2 Come, tenderest Friend, and best,
  Our most delightful Guest,
    With soothing power:
  Rest, which the weary know,
  Shade, 'mid the noontide glow,
  Peace, when deep griefs o'erflow,
    Cheer us, this hour!

3 Come, Light serene, and still
  Our inmost bosoms fill;
    Dwell in each breast;
  We know no dawn but thine,
  Send forth thy beams divine,
  On our dark souls to shine,
    And make us blest!

4 Come, all the faithful bless;
  Let all who Christ confess
    His praise employ;
  Give virtue's rich reward;
  Victorious death accord,
  And, with our glorious Lord,
    Eternal joy!

ROBERT II., KING OF FRANCE (972 — 1031).
Tr. by R. PALMER.

1 Lift your glad voices in triumph on high,
   For Jesus hath risen, and man shall not die;
   Vain were the terrors that gathered around him,
   And short the dominion of death and the grave;
   He burst from the fetters of darkness that bound him,
   Resplendent in glory, to live and to save:
   Loud was the chorus of angels on high,—
   The Saviour hath risen, and man shall not die.

2 Glory to God, in full anthems of joy;
   The being he gave us, death cannot destroy:
   Sad were the life we may part with to-morrow,
   If tears were our birthright, and death were our end;
   But Jesus hath cheered the dark valley of sorrow,
   And bade us, immortal, to heaven ascend:
   Lift then your voices in triumph on high,
   For Jesus hath risen, and man shall not die.

            Rev. HENRY WARE, Jr., D.D. (1793—1843).

No. 104. THE STAR OF THE EAST. 11s, 10s.

KIALMARK.

1 Brightest and best of the sons of the morning,
   Dawn on our darkness, and lend us thine aid;
 Star of the East, the horizon adorning,
   Guide where our infant Redeemer is laid.
 Cold on his cradle the dewdrops are shining;
   Low lies his bed with the beasts of the stall;
 Angels adore Him, in slumber reclining,—
   Maker, and Monarch, and Saviour of all.

2 Say, shall we yield him, in costly devotion,
   Odors of Edom and offerings divine?
 Gems of the mountain, and pearls of the ocean,
   Myrrh from the forest, and gold from the mine?
 Vainly we offer each ample oblation;
   Vainly with gifts would his favor secure;
 Richer by far is the heart's adoration;
   Dearer to God are the prayers of the poor.

BISHOP REGINALD HEBER, D.D. (1783—   ).

No. 105. THY WILL BE DONE. (Chant.)

H. Schwing (1825—).

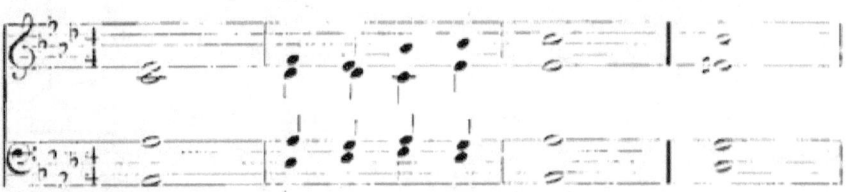
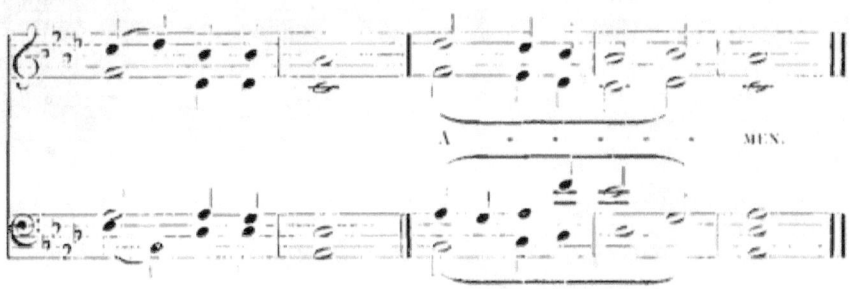

1 Father, I know thy ways are just,
   Although to me unknown;
   O grant me grace thy love to trust,
   And cry, " Thy will be done."

2 If thou shouldst hedge with thorns my path,
   Should wealth and friends be gone;
   Still, with a firm and lively faith,
   I'll cry, " Thy will be done."

3 Although thy steps I cannot trace,
   Thy sovereign right I'll own;
   And, as instructed by thy grace,
   I'll cry, " Thy will be done."

4 'T is sweet thus passively to lie
   Before thy gracious throne,
   Concerning everything to cry,
   " My Father's will be done."

No. 106. SHALL WE MEET BEYOND THE RIVER? (Chant.)

UNKNOWN.

1 Shall we meet be- | yond the | river, |
   Where the surges | cease to | roll? |
   Where the blessed | sing for | ever,
   Songs that fill the | raptured | soul? |
   Shall we meet? | Yes! be- | yond the | river.

2 Shall we meet with | all the | loved ones, |
   That were torn from | our em | brace? |
   Shall we listen | to their | voices, |
   And behold them | face to | face? |
   Shall we meet? | Yes! be- | yond the | river.

3 Shall we meet with | Christ our | Saviour, |
   When he comes to | claim his | own? |
   Shall we know his | blessed | favor, |
   And behold him | on his | throne? |
   Shall we meet? | Yes! be- | yond the | river.

No. 107. BEYOND! (Chant.)

W. A. Tarbutton (1817—1885).

Love, rest and home, sweet home! Lord, tar-ry not, but come.

1 Beyond the smiling and the weeping, |
   I shall be | soon;
  Beyond the waking and the sleeping, |
  Beyond the sowing and the reaping, |
   I shall be | soon.

2 Beyond the blooming and the fading, |
   I shall be | soon;
  Beyond the shining and the shading, |
  Beyond the hoping and the dreading |
   I shall be | soon.

3 Beyond the rising and the setting, |
   I shall be | soon;
  Beyond the calming and the fretting, |
  Beyond remembering and forgetting. |
   I shall be | soon.

4 Beyond the parting and the meeting, |
   I shall be | soon;
  Beyond the farewell and the greeting |
  Beyond the pulse's fever beating, |
   I shall be | soon.

5 Beyond the frost-chain and the fever, |
   I shall be | soon;
  Beyond the rock-waste and the river, |
  Beyond the ever and the never. |
   I shall be | soon.

No. 108. NEARER, MY GOD, TO THEE! (Chant.)

HENRY SCHWING (1825—).

1 Nearer, my God, to thee, |
   Nearer to | thee!
E'en though it be a cross
   That | raiseth | me;
Still all my | song shall | be, |
   Nearer, my | God, to | thee,
   Nearer to | thee!

2 Though like a wanderer, |
   The | sun gone | down,
Darkness be over me,
   My | rest a | stone;
Yet in my | dreams I'd | be
   Nearer, my | God, to | thee,
   Nearer to | thee.

3 There let the way appear, |
   Steps unto heaven;
All that thou sendest me,
   In | mercy | given;
Angels to | beckon | me
   Nearer, my | God to | thee.
   Nearer to | thee!

4 Then, with my waking thoughts, |
   Bright with thy | praise,
Out of my stony griefs, |
   Bethel I'll | raise;
So by my | woes to | be
   Nearer, my | God, to | thee.
   Nearer to | thee.

5 Or if on joyful wing, |
   Cleaving the sky,
Sun, moon, and stars forgot |
   Upward I | fly;
Still all my | song shall | be,—
   Nearer, my | God, to | thee,
   Nearer to | thee!

Mrs. SARAH F. ADAMS (1805—1849).

No. 109.   DE PROFUNDIS.   (Chant.)

Ps. 130. (*Revised Version.*)

Arranged by Dr. W. H. HOPKINS.

1 Out of the depths have I cried unto |
      thee, O | Lord.‖
   Lord, | hear my | voice. ‖
   Let thine ears be attentive |
      To the | voice |
   Of my | suppli- | cations. ‖

2 If thou, Lord, shouldest |
      Mark in- | iquities, |
   O Lord, | who shall | stand ? ‖
   But there is forgiveness |
      With— | thee, ‖
   That thou | mayest be | feared. ‖

3 I wait for the Lord, my |
      Soul doth | wait, ‖
   And in his word | do I | hope. ‖
   My soul looketh for the Lord more than
      watchmen look |
      For the | morning. ‖
   Yea, more than watchmen |
      For the | morning. ‖

4 O Israel, hope in the Lord; for with the
      There is | mercy, ‖   { Lord |
   And with him is | plenteous re- | demp-
      tion. ‖
   And he shall re- | deem— | Israel |
   From | all his in- | iquities. ‖ A-MEN.

No. 110.　　　COME TO ME.　(Chant.)

UNKNOWN.

1 With tearful eyes I look around,
　　Life seems a dark and *stormy* sea;
　Yet, 'midst the gloom, I hear a sound,
　　A heavenly *whisper:* "Come to me."

2 It tells me of a place of rest—
　　It tells me where my *soul may* flee;
　Oh! to the weary, faint, oppressed,
　　How sweet the *bidding:* "Come to me."

3 When nature shudders, loth to part
　　From all I love, *enjoy and* see,
　When a faint chill steals o'er my heart,
　　A sweet voice *utters:* "Come to me."

4 Come, for all else must fade and die,
　　Earth is no resting *place for* thee;
　Heavenward direct thy weeping eye,
　　I am thy *portion:* "Come to me."

5 O voice of mercy! voice of love!
　　In conflict, grief and *agony,*
　Support me, cheer me from above!
　　And gently *whisper:* "Come to me."

(110)

No. 111. GLORIA PATRI. (Chant.)

HENRY SCHWING.

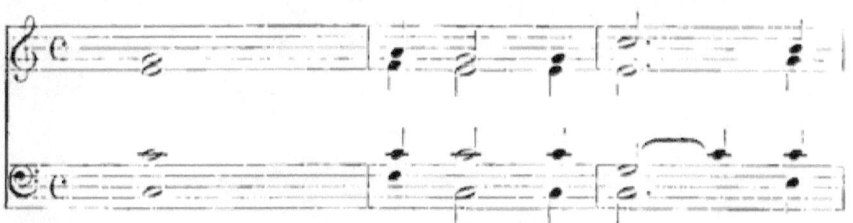

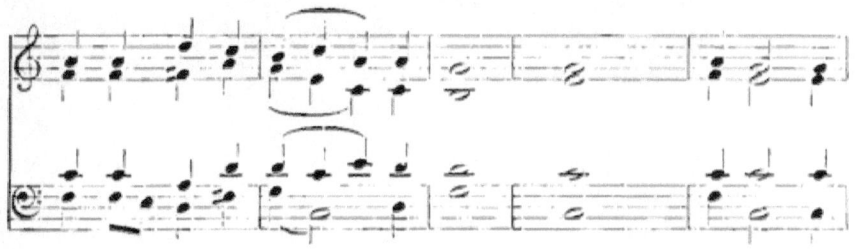

Glory be to the | Father,
And | to the | Son,
And to the | Holy | Ghost; |
As it was in the be- | ginning,
Is | now and ' ever shall be, |
World without | end. A | men.

METRICAL INDEX.

	NO.
America. 6s & 4s	77
America. 6s & 4s	78
Amsterdam. 7s & 6s	79
Angelus. 8s & 7s, 6 lines	69
Antioch. C. M.	2
Ariel. C. P. M.	80
Arlington. C. M.	3
Austria. 8s & 7s, Double	68
Autumn. 8s & 7s, Double	70
Azmon. C. M.	4
Balerma. C. M.	5
Barby. C. M.	6
Bartlett. 7s	56
Bennett. 7s, Double	57
Beyond. (Chant)	107
Chant	85
Come to Me	110
Coronation. C. M.	7
Coventry. C. M.	8
De Profundis (Chant)	109
Dennis. S. M.	46
Diademata. S. M. Double	47
Duke Street. L. M.	24
Dulcetta. 8s & 7s	71
Dundee. C. M.	9
Eventide. 10s	84
Ewing. 7s, 6 lines	58

	NO.
Fisher. 7s, 6 lines	59
Fortress. 8s, 7s, & 6s	81
Germany. L. M.	25
Gloria Patri (Chant)	111
Goucher. 7s, 6 lines	61
Greenville. 8s, 7s, & 4s	86
Hamburg. L. M.	23
Heidelberg. C. M.	10
Hendon. 7s	62
Holy Cross. C. M.	11
Hope. L. M.	28
Hopkins. S. M. Double	48
Horton. 7s	60
Hursley. L. M.	29
In the Hour of Trial. 6s & 5s	82
In the Silent Midnight Watches. 8s & 5s	89
Italian Hymn. 6s & 4s	90
Jennie. 8s & 7s	72
Jewett. 6s	87
Lanesboro. C. M.	12
Litany Hymn. 7s, 8 lines	63
Louvan. L. M.	30
Lyons. 10s & 11s	92
Manoah. C. M.	13
Mary. 10s, 4 lines	83

METRICAL INDEX.

	NO.		NO.
Mear. C. M.	15	Shall We Meet (Chant).	106
Mendon. L. M.	31	Shelloe. L. M. 6 lines	39
Mercy Seat. L. M.	32	Shelly. S. M.	55
Mornington. S. M.	49	Shirland. S. M.	52
Mozart. C. M.	16	Shontz. C. M.	71
		Sicilian Hymn. 8s & 7s.	74
Naille. S. M.	50	Silver Street. S. M.	53
Naomi. C. M.	18	Simpson. C. M.	20
Nearer, my God, to Thee	108	Spencer. L. M.	40
Nicea. 11s, 12s. & 10s.	93	Spohr. C. M. Double	21
Nuremberg. 7s	64	Star of the East (The) 11s & 10s.	104
		St. Agnes. C. M.	1
O Holy Saviour. 8s. 8s, 8s. & 5s	88	St. Helen. L. M.	27
Old Hundred	34	St. Martin's. C. M.	14
Onward. 6s & 5s	94	St. Paul's	97
O Sacred Head. 7s & 6s	95	St. Thomas. S. M.	54
Park Street. L. M.	35	Thy Will Be Done (Chant)	105
Paradise. 8s, 6s, & 6s	98	Trumpet. 10s, 11s. & 12s	103
Pax Dei. 11s & 10s	96	Truro. L. M.	41
Pleyel's Hymn. 7s	65		
Portuguese Hymn. 11s.	99	Van Meter. L. M. Double.	42
Praise. L. M.	36		
Prayer. 8s, 8s, 8s, & 4s	100	Warwick. C. M.	22
Promise. L. M.	37	Webb. 7s & 6s	91
		Wesley. L. M.	45
Rathbun. 8s & 7s	73	Wilcox. 8s & 7s. Double	75
Regent Square. 8s, 7s. & 4s. 6 lines	101	Wilman. L. M.	33
Reminiscence. L. M.	38	Wilmot. 8s & 7s	76
Repose. 7s. 6 lines	66	Wilson. L. M. 6 lines	44
Righini. 6s & 4s	102	Worthington. 8s & 7s	67
Salvation. C. M. Double	19	Zerah. C. M.	23
Selvin. S. M.	51		

INDEX OF FIRST LINES.

	NO.		NO.
All hail the power of Jesus' name	7	God is love; his mercy brightens	73
A mighty fortress is our God	81	God moves in a mysterious way	9
As pants the wearied hart	83	Had I the gift of tongues	54
As shadows, cast by cloud and sun	14	Happy the man who finds the grace	31
As with gladness men of old	59	Hark, my soul! it is the Lord	56
As with gladness men of old	61	Hark! what mean those holy voices	76
Awake, and sing the song	52	Head of the church whose spirit fills	87
		He leadeth me! O blessed thought	42
Before Jehovah's awful throne	34	Holy as thou, O Lord, is none	26
Behold the throne of grace	55	Holy, holy, holy, Lord God Almighty	93
Beyond the smiling and the weeping	107	Holy Spirit, Truth Divine	64
Blest hour, when mortal man retires	33	Honor and glory, thanksgiving	84
Brightest and best of the sons	104	How beauteous are their feet	51
		How firm a foundation	99
Chief of sinners though I be	66		
Christ is coming! let creation	86	If, on a quiet sea	46
Come, Holy Ghost, in love	102	I heard the voice of Jesus say	21
Come, let us tune our loftiest song	41	In the hour of trial	82
Come, sound his praise abroad	53	In the silent midnight watches	89
Come unto me, when shadows	96	It is not death to die	50
Crown him with many crowns	47	It may not be our lot to wield	24
		I was a wandering sheep	48
Faith of our fathers, living still	44	I will praise thee, Sun of Glory	69
Father, I know thy ways are just	105		
Father of heaven, whose love profound	45	Jerusalem the golden	58
From every stormy wind that blows	32	Jesus, Lover of my soul	57
		Jesus my Advocate above	25
Glorious things of thee are spoken	68	Jesus, my Truth, my Way	49
Glory be to the Father	111	Jesus, the sinners' Friend, to thee	28
Glory be to God on high	60	Jesus, the very thought of thee	12
		Jesus, thou joy of loving hearts	35

INDEX OF FIRST LINES.

First Line	NO.
Joy to the world! the Lord is come	2
Just as I am, without one plea	45
Laboring and heavy laden	71
Let every tongue thy goodness speak	23
Lift up your heads, ye mighty gates	30
Lift your glad voices in triumph	103
Lord, as to thy dear cross we flee	18
Lord, in the morning thou shalt hear	22
Lord of all being! throned afar	29
Love divine, all love excelling	74
Love divine, all love excelling	75
My country! 't is of thee	77
My God, is any hour so sweet	100
My hope is built on nothing less	39
My Saviour on the word of truth	19
Nearer, my God, to thee	105
Never further than Thy cross	65
New every morning is the love	27
	36
O Christ, who hast prepared a place	38
O come, Creator, Spirit blest	40
O could I speak the matchless worth	80
O for a heart to praise my God	4
O God, to thee we raise our eyes	37
Oh, it is hard to work for God	15
O holy Saviour, Friend unseen	88
O Jesus, King most wonderful	11
Onward, Christian soldiers	94
O Paradise! O Paradise	98
O sacred Head, now wounded	95
O Sun of righteousness, arise	5
O Thou God of my salvation	101
Out of the depths have I cried	109

First Line	NO.
Praise the Lord! ye heavens adore him	72
Prayer is the breath of God in man	17
Rise, glorious Conqueror, rise	90
Rise, my soul, and stretch thy wings	79
Safely through another week	61
Saviour, again to thy dear Name	84
Saviour, when, in dust, to Thee	63
Shall we meet beyond the river	106
Sing with all the sons of glory	70
Stand up, stand up, for Jesus	91
Sweet is the work, my God, my King	36
The counsels of redeeming grace	16
The glorious universe around	8
There is an eye that never sleeps	3
There is a safe and secret place	6
There 's a wideness in God 's mercy	67
They who seek the throne of grace	62
Thine forever, God of love	60
Thou art the way:—to thee alone	20
Thou, whose almighty word	78
Thy way, not mine, O Lord	87
Thou Lamb of God, thou Prince of Peace	36
Walk in the light, so shalt thou know	10
Wave, wave the Banner	97
We may not climb the heavenly steps	13
With tearful eyes I look	110
Workman of God: O lose not heart	1
When time seems short and death is near	44
Ye servants of God, your master	92

www.ingramcontent.com/pod-product-compliance
Lightning Source LLC
Chambersburg PA
CBHW020123170426
43199CB00009B/608